The Poems of Jonathan Swift

The Poems of Jonathan Swift

Selected, with an Introduction
by Padraic Colum

 COLLIER BOOKS   NEW YORK

COLLIER-MACMILLAN LTD   LONDON

Library of Congress Catalog Card Number: 61-18573

First Edition 1962

SECOND PRINTING 1967

The Macmillan Company, New York
Collier-Macmillan Canada Ltd., Toronto, Ontario
Printed in the United States of America

Table of Contents

INTRODUCTION 9

SWIFT AMONG HIS FRIENDS 17

The Dean's Manner of Living 17

Twelve Articles 17

To A Lady 18

Stella At Wood Park 25

Market Women's Cries 28

Riddles 29

Mrs. Frances Harris's Petition 33

The Description of an Irish Feast 36

Baucis and Philemon 39

To Stella 44

Stella's Birth-Day 48

To Betty, The Grisette 50

My Lady's Lamentation and Complaint
Against the Dean 51

A Panegyric on the Dean 57

Addressed to the Earl of Oxford, Prime
Minister of England 65

On the Death of Dr. Swift 69

Stella to Dr. Swift 81

CADENUS AND VANESSA 83

SWIFT AND MANKIND 105

A Description of the Morning 105

An Elegy 106

The Description of a Salamander 107

A Beautiful Young Nymph Going to Bed 109

Phyllis 111

The Progress of Poetry 114

Helter Skelter 116

The Progress of Marriage 118

An Excellent New Ballad 122

In Sickness 124

The Day of Judgment 125

SWIFT'S EPITAPH 126

The Poems of Jonathan Swift

Introduction

A PRESENT-DAY EDITOR of Swift's poetical pieces has to be ready with an answer to a question: Can you entitle the collection *The Poems of Jonathan Swift?* The question is begged by the word *poems*. For us *poem* means a regularly rhythmical piece that is charged with emotion, that reaches beyond the rational into the imaginative, that transports us from the here and now. When Swift wrote one of his rhymed pieces, he did not go beyond the rational, made no attempt to transport us, and kept his emotion subordinate to the effect that he wanted to produce. What his object was in writing verse he left on record:

> True poets can depress and raise
> Are lords of infamy and praise,
> They are not scurrilous in satire,
> Nor will in panegyric flatter.
> Unjustly poets we asperse;
> Truth shines the brighter clad in verse,
> And all the fictions they pursue
> Do but insinuate what is true.

The function of poetry is social; it makes truth, social truth, shine; it differs from prose, which carries an argument, in the fact that it insinuates and, thereby, evades the possibility of rejection. Stated like this, Swift and we—and when we name him we name all his great contemporaries—do not mean the same thing when we use the word *poem* or *poetry*.

Having said this, we have to say something else: The work so conceived had to have design and workmanship. It had to be informed by a mind that was trained and alert. In no other age was loose thinking, slovenly workmanship, failure in structure, grammatical ignorance so mercilessly assailed. The poet was one who made a meaningful construction in language that was heightened by the rigor of form. Swift, with the power of projecting a personality, with the mastery of a form he chooses to use, produces something memorable when he writes what are to him poems. May we not speak of these memorable things as poems? Yes, for assuredly something has been created in metrical language. Objective, discounting emotion, refusing to transport us from the here and now, these pieces by virtue of their creative force make place for themselves in some category of poetry.

The most widely circulated of prose writers—at least in the case of one of his books—Swift for a long time has been kept out of the canon of poetry in English. True, there is no reason why we should suppose a master of prose can express himself in a masterly way in verse. And yet, the volume of his verse is so great that we have to think it odd that none of the standard anthologies were able to discover a few usable pieces. "The Day of Judgment," to mention one, is an unforgettable poem. Certain special poems of Swift's have appeared in recent Irish anthologies, but by and large his name is unknown to readers of poetry. Collections have been published, but they have been directed towards the universities. The present selection comes out of another intention: It is intended for the people who make the audience for our twentieth century poets.

"He always understands himself, and his readers understand him," Samuel Johnson wrote about Swift's work generally. When we apply this dictum to his poetry we see what limits it sets up. The poet must transcend himself, we believe; as readers we expect that we will not immediately understand, or, rather, that in what the poet writes or repeats to us, there will be something left over for us to speculate on. In Swift there is nothing left over. We are left in immediate possession of the whole of his intention.

> She walks in beauty like the night
> Of cloudless climes and starry skies.

Here we feel that the poet has gone beyond himself, and we are not sure that he understands what he is saying. An experience of the kind is not in Swift's world.

What, then, do we, thinking of poetry, go into that world for? Well, perhaps to see the here and now being made significant, the occasional being given a permanence, but mainly to share in the projections of an extraordinarily forceful and energetic mind. And in doing this we get away from a modernity in which poetry has become private, intensely subjective, disdainful of ordinary meaning, concerned with the distant, delighting in the enigmatic, passing into the meaningless. This complete objectivity, this actuality of situation, can come to us as something tonic.

And there is something that is quite exceptional in Swift's poetry. I am inclined to name it as his power of producing "audience participation." In his unformed years he went through collections of street-songs that were in Trinity College, Dublin, that bore such titles as *The Newest and Most Ingenious Poems, Songs, Catches, etc., Against Popery* (1689), *The Muse's Farewell to Popery and Slavery* (1690), *Poems on Affairs of State* (1703), and *A Collection of Poems Relating to State Affairs* (1705). Such pieces were made to influence crowds, to down adversaries, and, no doubt, were in a style popular enough to set apprentice boys singing them. What the makers of such songs try to do is to bring the audience into the situation.

Swift practiced their method. His practice is shown in the songs he wrote to be sung in the streets during his campaign against the valueless currency being put over on Ireland—Wood's ha'pence. And on another occasion and on a level more characteristic of himself there is "The True English Dean to Be Hanged for a Rape." With the power of producing "audience participation" which, I think, he learnt from the street song, he has another power which seems to me to be as exceptional: a faculty of judgment. I will try to be precise about this: We seldom put much of our being into knowing a thing and deciding on its worth. Swift can do it. His decision may not be fair, but it is a decision. And there is another quality which makes his poems remarkable; it is mentioned by Goldsmith in what I believe to be one of the rare pieces of genuine criticism of Swift's poems. His poetry is distinguished, Goldsmith said, not by its greatness, but by its boldness. Boldness is a seldom-found quality in verse; it is present in nearly every verse of Swift's that we read. Often he begins in the spirit of a man attacking someone; the attack usually astounds us not only by its boldness but by its dexterity.

More than any other poet, Swift had the power of projecting his personality. He was born with a dramatic talent. His "Polite Conversations" show he could be a dramatist if the intrigue which was the feature of the eighteenth-century comedy had not been too dull for him. Perhaps

11

it would be truer to say he had a genius for stage management: This genius is shown in the way he built up the issue of Wood's ha'pence to a towering climax—the hidden man who attracts loyalty, the accompaniment of street songs, the muffling of the bells of St. Patrick's on the condemnation of the *Drapier's Letters,* the inevitable advance to a higher statement—the independence of Ireland. And in his private poems he does what writers are seldom able to do: He dramatizes himself as a character—"Swift," "the Doctor," and, most sympathetic of all, "the Dean." He sees himself as seen through other people's eyes; his most charming pieces are the ones in which he sees himself through women's eyes as the rather exacting companion.

I have used a word about Swift's poetry which most people who have read the bulk of it will hear with much surprise—the word *charming*. The words they would be most inclined to use are *coarse, brutal, filthy*. And certainly these words characterize a great deal of it. What is one to say about the poem that has the title "A Beautiful Young Nymph Going to Bed"? Is it enough to say that it is just heartless? Swift, later on, will say about himself:

> For he abhorred the senseless tribe
> Who call it humour when they gibe:
> He spared the hump and crooked nose
> Whose owners set not up for beaux.

But here he is pursuing with disgrace a starving, sick street-walker:

> Corinna, pride of Drury-Lane,
> For whom no shepherd sighs in vain.

Perhaps in humiliating the poor creature he is humiliating himself as a member of the human race. But how could he have kept it up through all those lines in which ignominy is heaped on ignominy? Perhaps there is an excuse in saying that Swift wanted to confront the fashionable versifiers of the pastoral with the realities of the metropolitan. Nymphs and shepherds indeed! He tosses all that out when he takes the bedraggled Corinna up the four flights of stairs to her dismal tenement:

> No drunken rake to pick her up,
> No cellar where on tick to sup.

In the centre of Swift's poetical output is the peculiar "Cadenus and Vanessa. It is a poem that was written on demand. In London a young woman of the type that to-day we would call a "society girl" fell in love with the middle-aged Doctor Swift. In Dublin was the elder Stella to whom he was bound in honor, affection, habit, mutual understanding. "Another land, another love" is a not unusual occurrence. Ideally, the party on the other side of the frontier should surrender claims. But this young lady — Hester Vanhomrigh was her name — was terrifyingly modern. She was her own mistress; she was self-willed; she was in love with the man of affairs who describes himself as having grown old in politics and wit. When he returned to take up the deanship of St. Patrick's she followed him to Ireland. This is as much of the story as we need to know when we read "Cadenus and Vanessa."

The least a poet can do is to give an exacting girl the tribute of a poem. Swift, in doing this, uses a mythological machinery which to us is cumbersome. For all his invention and wit, the poem brings Vanessa over to us as a pedant and a prude. There is melancholy in the presentation of the elderly Cadenus:

> But books, and time, and state affairs,
> Had spoil'd his fashionable airs:
> He now could praise, esteem, approve,
> But understood not what was love.

The end, too, is melancholy. The young woman declares her passion to the man who at forty-four regards himself as elderly:

> The nymph will have her turn to be
> The tutor; and the pupil, he;
> Though she already can discern
> Her scholar is not apt to learn;
> Or wants capacity to reach
> The science she designs to teach.

It is a long poem, about nine hundred lines. Swift, who was so well able to project himself, only peers out of it. Vanessa comes out as a spoiled youngster, a brat, if ever there was one. It is a poem written by a courtier to a demanding beauty whom he distrusts—on the emotional level, anyway. The poet of "Cadenus and Vanessa" describes himself "grown old in politics and wit." And that is what the poem is compounded of: politics, the politics of the not-quite-committed lover; and wit, the conscious mind making a memorial of the experience, and elevating it.

Jonathan Swift's poems, with few exceptions, are occasional: They come, not out of prolonged contemplation, but out of some happening, some situation that the poet finds himself in, and the fact that they are occasional, even casual—there are over four hundred pieces in the collection I have used—gives them a singular impact: the voice, the gesture of a person comes over to us. In his letters to an Irish officer in the French service, the Chevalier Wogan, he speaks of his verses as being trifles. That was a description that he used in passing. We may be sure that the man who looked on himself as born to introduce irony would not want these innovating pieces to be set aside as trifles. Few were printed in his lifetime; he never saw a published collection. His Stella collected and transcribed the poems he had written up to that time (but the politic Dean must have kept some from her attention). He approved of her labor:

> So, if this pile of scattered rhymes
> Should be approved in after times;
> If it both pleases and endures,
> The merit and the praise are yours.

I have spoken of Swift's power to project himself. The greatest of these projections is carved in black marble in St. Patrick's Cathedral, and it is in Latin. It tells generations that he has gone where savage indignation can no longer lacerate his heart. It is addressed to the traveller who will come before it. The Traveller! His most famous book takes its title from a traveller—*Gulliver's Travels*. His poem often gives the impression of an arrival, of a man who has just come on the scene:

Amazed, confused, its fate unknown,
The world stood trembling at his throne.

A scene is being witnessed. The *Journal to Stella* begins
with an arrival and is mainly about arrivals. Jonathan
Swift is a man who arrives, sees, judges. And the impression we get is not due to chance, the impression of a man
in transit. Swift's centre is neither England nor Ireland. He
was Irish by birth, but English by infantile surroundings;
Irish by boyhood and youth, then English by young manhood; Irish again; then English by participation in great
affairs; then Irish again by championing an Irish cause, a
cause which had to do, not merely with a political job,
Mr. Wood and his ha'pence, but with the dignity of the
Irish Kingdom. In the *Drapier's Letters* he names himself
an Irishman, but with ambiguity.

When, in St. Patrick's Cathedral in Dublin, we stand
before the black marble on which his epitaph is inscribed,
we know that a man has been here and has found a way
of making the generations know it. Yeats has made an
unforgettable poem out of the epitaph, concluding—

> Imitate him if you dare,
> World-besotted traveller; he
> Served human liberty.

It is not exactly what Swift had inscribed: his appeal was
not to a "world-besotted traveller." It was to a traveller.

In poetry, his greatest projection of himself is "On the
Death of Dean Swift." Here he is the man who, although
denied his proper dues, made himself the champion of a
country and the champion of his friends. It is a poem
about judgment, judgment on himself as a public character. He judges his own writings, in particular the
Drapier's Letters, knows that they have had what he
wanted them to have, public influence, knows that they
are not neglected. His poetry was original and originating:

> His vein, ironically grave,
> Exposed the fool and lashed the knave,
> To steal a hint was never known,
> But what he writ was all his own.

About the arrangement of the poems in this collection a word has to be said. Out of over four hundred pieces, forty have been chosen. In their placing, chronology has been left out of account; later poems or earlier follow or preceed each other. And in making a selection and an arrangement, a problem in editorship had to be dealt with. Swift standardized his verse forms and refused to move towards any wide range of subject. But it is only fair to readers to exhibit what diversity he has. I have tried to do this. As for the larger arrangement, it is in accordance with the polarity in Swift's mind: He liked persons in particular and he hated the generality of mankind. I recognize the division in his mind and I make the division in this collection according to it: "Swift Among His Friends" and "Swift and Mankind." Between is interposed "Cadenus and Vanessa."

PADRAIC COLUM.

Dublin, January 1961

Swift Among His Friends

The Dean's Manner of Living

On rainy days alone I dine
Upon a chick and pint of wine.
On rainy days I dine alone,
And pick my chicken to the bone;
But this my servants much enrages,
No scraps remain to save board-wages.
In weather fine I nothing spend,
But often spunge upon a friend;
Yet, where he's not so rich as I,
I pay my club, and so good b'ye.

Twelve Articles

I

Lest it may more quarrels breed,
I will never hear you read.

II

By disputing, I will never,
To convince you once endeavour.

III

When a paradox you stick to,
I will never contradict you.

IV

When I talk and you are heedless,
I will show no anger needless.

V

When your speeches are absurd,
I will ne'er object a word.

VI

When you furious argue wrong,
I will grieve and hold my tongue.

VII

Not a jest or humorous story
Will I ever tell before ye:
To be chidden for explaining,
When you quite mistake the meaning.

VIII

Never more will I suppose,
You can taste my verse or prose.

IX

You no more at me shall fret,
While I teach and you forget.

X

You shall never hear me thunder,
When you blunder on, and blunder.

XI

Show your poverty of spirit,
And in dress place all your merit;
Give yourself ten thousand airs:
That with me shall break no squares.

XII

Never will I give advice,
Till you please to ask me thrice:
Which if you in scorn reject,
'Twill be just as I expect.

Thus we both shall have our ends,
And continue special friends.

To A Lady

who desired the Author to write some
Verses upon her in the Heroic Style

After venting all my spite,
Tell me, what have I to write?
Every error I could find
Through the mazes of your mind,
Have my busy Muse employ'd,
Till the company was cloy'd.

Are you positive and fretful,
Heedless, ignorant, forgetful?
Those, and twenty follies more,
I have often told before.

Hearken what my lady says:
Have I nothing then to praise?
Ill it fits you to be witty,
Where a fault should move your pity.
If you think me too conceited,
Or to passion quickly heated;
If my wandering head be less
Set on reading, than on dress;
If I always seem too dull t'ye;
I can solve the diffi-culty.

You would teach me to be wise:
Truth and honour how to prize;
How to shine in conversation,
And with credit fill my station;
How to relish notions high;
How to live, and how to die.

But it was decreed by Fate—
Mr. Dean, you come too late.
Well I know, you can discern,
I am now too old to learn:
Follies from my youth instill'd,
Have my soul entirely fill'd;
In my head and heart they centre,
Nor will let your lessons enter.

Bred a fondling and an heiress;
Drest like any lady mayoress:
Cocker'd by the servants round,
Was too good to touch the ground;
Thought the life of every lady
Should be one continued play-day—
Balls and masquerades, and shows,
Visits, plays, and powder'd beaux.

Thus you have my case at large,
And may now perform your charge.
Those materials I have furnish'd,
When by you refin'd and burnish'd,
Must, that all the world may know 'em,
Be reduced into a poem.
But, I beg, suspend a while
That same paltry, burlesque style;

Drop for once your constant rule,
Turning all to ridicule,
Teaching others how to ape you;
Court nor parliament can 'scape you;
Treat the public and your friends
Both alike, while neither mends.
  Sing my praise in strain sublime:
Treat me not with dogg'rel rhyme.
'Tis but just you should produce,
With each fault, each fault's excuse;
Not to publish every trifle,
And my few perfections stifle.
With some gifts at least endow me,
Which my very foes allow me.
Am I spiteful, proud, unjust?
Did I ever break my trust?
Which of all our modern dames
Censures less, or less defames?
In good manners am I faulty?
Can you call me rude or haughty?
Did I e'er my mite withhold
From the impotent and old?
When did ever I omit
Due regard for men of wit?
When have I esteem express'd
For a coxcomb gaily dress'd?
Do I, like the female tribe,
Think it wit to fleer and gibe?
Who, with less designing ends,
Kindlier entertains her friends;
With good words and countenance sprightly,
Strives to treat them more politely?
  Think not cards my chief diversion:
'Tis a wrong, unjust aspersion:
Never knew I any good in 'em,
But to dose my head like laudanum.
We, by play, as men, by drinking,
Pass our nights to drive out thinking.
From my ailments give me leisure,
I shall read and think with pleasure;
Conversation learn to relish,
And with books my mind embellish.
  Now, methinks, I hear you cry,
Mr. Dean, you must reply.

Madam, I allow 'tis true:
All these praises are your due.
You, like some acute philosopher,
Every fault have drawn a gloss over;
Placing in the strongest light
All your virtues to my sight.

Though you lead a blameless life,
Are a humble prudent wife,
Answer all domestic ends:
What is this to us your friends?
Though your children by a nod
Stand in awe without a rod;
Though, by your obliging sway,
Servants love you, and obey;
Though you treat us with a smile;
Clear your looks, and smooth your style;
Load our plates from every dish;
This is not the thing we wish.
Colonel . . . may be your debtor;
We expect employment better.
You must learn, if you would gain us,
With good sense to entertain us.

Scholars, when good sense describing,
Call it tasting and imbibing;
Metaphoric meat and drink
Is to understand and think;
We may carve for others thus;
And let others carve for us;
To discourse, and to attend,
Is, to help yourself and friend.
Conversation is but carving;
Carve for all, yourself is starving;
Give no more to every guest,
Than he's able to digest;
Give him always of the prime;
And but little at a time.
Carve to all but just enough:
Let them neither starve nor stuff.
And, that you may have your due,
Let your neighbours carve for you.
This comparison will hold,
Could it well in rhyme be told,
How conversing, listening, thinking,
Justly may resemble drinking;

For a friend a glass you fill,
What is this but to instil?
  To conclude this long essay;
Pardon if I disobey,
Nor against my natural vein,
Treat you in heroic strain.
I, as all the parish knows,
Hardly can be grave in prose:
Still to lash, and lashing smile,
Ill befits a lofty style.
From the planet of my birth
I encounter vice with mirth.
Wicked ministers of state
I can easier scorn than hate;
And I find it answers right:
Scorn torments them more than spite.
All the vices of a court
Do but serve to make me sport.
Were I in some foreign realm,
Which all vices overwhelm;
Should a monkey wear a crown,
Must I tremble at his frown?
Could I not, through all his ermine,
'Spy the strutting, chattering vermin;
Safely write a smart lampoon,
To expose the brisk baboon?
  When my Muse officious ventures
On the nation's representers:
Teaching by what golden rules
Into knaves they turn their fools;
How the helm is ruled by Walpole,
At whose oars, like slaves, they all pull;
Let the vessel split on shelves;
With the freight enrich themselves;
Safe within my little wherry,
All their madness makes me merry:
Like the waterman of Thames,
I row by, and call them names;
Like the ever-laughing sage,
In a jest I spend my rage:
(Though it must be understood
I would hang them if I could;)
If I can but fill my niche,
I attempt no higher pitch;

Leave to d'Anvers and his mate
Maxims wise to rule the state.
Pulteney deep, accomplish'd St. Johns,
Scourge the villains with a vengeance;
Let me, though the smell be noisome,
Strip their bums; let Caleb hoise 'em;
Then apply Alecto's whip
Till they wriggle, howl, and skip.

    Deuce is in you, Mr. Dean:
What can all this passion mean?
Mention courts! you'll ne'er be quiet
On corruptions running riot.
End as it befits your station;
Come to use and application;
Nor with senates keep a fuss.
I submit; and answer thus:

    If the machinations brewing,
To complete the public ruin,
Never once could have the power
To affect me half an hour;
Sooner would I write in buskins,
Mournful elegies on Blueskins.
If I laugh at Whig and Tory;
I conclude a fortiori,
All your eloquence will scarce
Drive me from my favourite farce.
This I must insist on; for, as
It is well observed by Horace,
Ridicule has greater power
To reform the world than sour.
Horses thus, let jockeys judge else,
Switches better guide than cudgels.
Bastings heavy, dry, obtuse,
Only dulness can produce;
While a little gentle jerking
Sets the spirits all a-working.

    Thus, I find it by experiment,
Scolding moves you less than merriment,
I may storm and rage in vain;
It but stupifies your brain.
But with raillery to nettle,
Sets your thoughts upon their mettle;
Gives imagination scope;
Never lets your mind elope;

Drives out brangling and contention,
Brings in reason and invention.
For your sake as well as mine,
I the lofty style decline.
I should make a figure scurvy,
And your head turn topsy-turvey.

I who love to have a fling
Both at senate-house and king:
That they might some better way tread,
To avoid the public hatred;
Thought no method more commodious
Than to show their vices odious;
Which I chose to make appear,
Not by anger, but by sneer.
As my method of reforming,
Is by laughing, not by storming,
(For my friends have always thought
Tenderness my greatest fault,)
Would you have me change my style?
On your faults no longer smile;
But, to patch up all our quarrels,
Quote you texts from Plutarch's Morals;
Or from Solomon produce
Maxims teaching Wisdom's use?

If I treat you like a crown'd head,
You have cheap enough compounded;
Can you put in higher claims
Than the owners of St. James?
You are not so great a grievance,
As the hirelings of St. Stephen's.
You are of a lower class
Than my friend Sir Robert Brass.
None of these have mercy found:
I have laugh'd, and lashed them round.

Have you seen a rocket fly?
You would swear it pierced the sky:
It but reached the middle air,
Bursting into pieces there;
Thousand sparkles falling down
Light on many a coxcomb's crown.
See what mirth the sport creates!
Singes hair, but breaks no pates.
Thus, should I attempt to climb,
Treat you in a style sublime,

Such a rocket is my Muse:
Should I lofty numbers choose,
Ere I reach'd Parnassus' top,
I should burst and bursting drop;
All my fire would fall in scraps,
Give your head some gentle raps;
Only make it smart a while;
Then could I forbear to smile,
When I found the tingling pain
Entering warm your frigid brain;
Make you able upon sight
To decide of wrong and right;
Talk with sense whate'er you please on;
Learn to relish truth and reason!
    Thus we both shall gain our prize;
I to laugh, and you grow wise.

Stella at Wood Park
A House of Charles Ford, Esq., near Dublin

Cuicumque nocere volebat,
Vestimenta dabat pretiosa.

Don Carlos, in a merry spite,
Did Stella to his house invite:
He entertain'd her half a year
With generous wines and costly cheer.
Don Carlos made her chief director,
That she might o'er the servants hector.
In half a week the dame grew nice,
Got all things at the highest price:
Now at the table head she sits,
Presented with the nicest bits:
She look'd on partridges with scorn,
Except they tasted of the corn:
A haunch of venison made her sweat,
Unless it had the right fumette.
Don Carlos earnestly would beg,
"Dear Madam, try this pigeon's leg";
Was happy, when he could prevail
To make her only touch a quail.
Through candle-light she view'd the wine,
To see that every glass was fine.
At last, grown prouder than the devil,

With feeding high, and treatment civil,
Don Carlos now began to find
His malice work as he design'd.
The winter sky began to frown:
Poor Stella must pack off to town;
From purling streams and fountains bubbling,
To Liffey's stinking tide in Dublin:
From wholesome exercise and air,
To sossing in an easy-chair:
From stomach sharp, and hearty feeding,
To piddle like a lady breeding,
From ruling there the household singly,
To be directed here by Dingley:
From every day a lordly banquet,
To half a joint, and God be thanked:
From every meal Pontack in plenty,
To half a pint one day in twenty:
From Ford attending at her call,
To visits of Archdeacon Wall
From Ford, who thinks of nothing mean,
To the poor doings of the Dean:
From growing richer with good cheer,
To running out by starving here.
  But now arrives the dismal day;
She must return to Ormond Quay.
The coachman stopt; she look'd, and swore
The rascal had mistook the door:
At coming in, you saw her stoop;
The entry brush'd against her hoop:
Each moment rising in her airs,
She curst the narrow winding stairs:
Began a thousand faults to spy;
The ceiling hardly six feet high;
The smutty wainscot full of cracks:
And half the chairs with broken backs;
Her quarter's out at Lady-day;
She vows she will no longer stay
In lodgings like a poor grisette,
While there are houses to be let.
  Howe'er, to keep her spirits up,
She sent for company to sup:
When all the while you might remark,
She strove in vain to ape Wood Park.
Two bottles call'd for, (half her store,

The cupboard could contain but four:)
A supper worthy of herself,
Five nothings in five plates of Delf.
 Thus for a week the farce went on;
When, all her country savings gone,
She fell into her former scene,
Small beer, a herring, and the Dean.
 Thus far in jest: though now, I fear,
You think my jesting too severe;
But poets, when a hint is new,
Regard not whether false or true:
Yet raillery gives no offence,
Where truth has not the least pretence;
Nor can be more securely placed
Than on a nymph of Stella's taste.
I must confess your wine and vittle
I was too hard upon a little:
Your table neat, your linen fine;
And, though in miniature, you shine:
Yet, when you sigh to leave Wood Park,
The scene, the welcome, and the spark,
To languish in this odious town,
And pull your haughty stomach down,
We think you quite mistake the case,
The virtue lies not in the place:
For though my raillery were true,
A cottage is Wood Park with you.

MARKET WOMEN'S CRIES

Apples

Come buy my fine wares,
Plums, apples, and pears.
A hundred a penny,
In conscience too many:
Come, will you have any?
My children are seven,
I wish them in Heaven;
My husband's a sot,
With his pipe and his pot,
Not a farthing will gain them,
And I must maintain them.

Asparagus

Ripe 'sparagras
Fit for lad or lass,
To make their water pass:
O, 'tis pretty picking
With a tender chicken!

Onions

Come, follow me by the smell,
Here are delicate onions to sell;
I promise to use you well.
They make the blood warmer,
You'll feed like a farmer;
For this is every cook's opinion,
No savoury dish without an onion;
But, lest your kissing should be spoil'd,
Your onions must be thoroughly boil'd:
Or else you may spare
Your mistress a share,
The secret will never be known:
She cannot discover
The breath of her lover,
But think it as sweet as her own.

Oysters

Charming oysters I cry:
My masters, come buy,
So plump and so fresh,
So sweet is their flesh,
No Colchester oyster
Is sweeter and moister:
Your stomach they settle,
And rouse up your mettle;
They'll make you a dad
Of a lass or a lad;
And madam your wife
They'll please to the life;
Be she barren, be she old,
Be she slut, or be she scold,
Eat my oysters, and lie near her,
She'll be fruitful, never fear her.

Herrings

Be not sparing,
Leave off swearing.
Buy my herring
Fresh from Malahide,
Better never was tried.
Come, eat 'em with pure fresh butter and mustard,
Their bellies are soft, and as white as a custard.
Come, sixpence a-dozen, to get me some bread,
Or, like my own herrings, I soon shall be dead.

Oranges

Come buy my fine oranges, sauce for your veal,
And charming, when squeezed in a pot of brown ale;
Well roasted, with sugar and wine in a cup,
They'll make a sweet bishop when gentlefolks sup.

RIDDLES

On Time

Ever eating, never cloying,
All-devouring, all-destroying,
Never finding full repast,
Till I eat the world at last.

On the Gallows

There is a gate, we know full well,
That stands 'twixt Heaven, and Earth, and Hell,
Where many for a passage venture,
Yet very few are found to enter:
Although 'tis open night and day,
They for that reason shun this way;
Both dukes and lords abhor its wood,
They can't come near it for their blood.
What other way they take to go,
Another time I'll let you know.
Yet commoners with greatest ease
Can find an entrance when they please.
The poorest hither march in state
(Or they can never pass the gate)
Like Roman generals triumphant,
And then they take a turn and jump on't.
If gravest parsons here advance,
They cannot pass before they dance;
There's not a soul that does resort here,
But strips himself to pay the porter.

On the Vowels

We are little airy creatures
All of different voice and features;
One of us in glass is set,
One of us you'll find in jet.
T'other you may see in tin,
And the fourth a box within.
If the fifth you should pursue,
It can never fly from you .

On Snow

From Heaven I fall, though from earth I begin,
No lady alive can show such a skin.
I'm bright as an angel, and light as a feather,
But heavy and dark, when you squeeze me together.
Though candour and truth in my aspect I bear,
Yet many poor creatures I help to ensnare.
Though so much of Heaven appears in my make,
The foulest impressions I easily take.
My parent and I produce one another,
The mother the daughter, the daughter the mother.

On a Cannon

Begotten, and born, and dying with noise,
The terror of woman, and pleasure of boys,
Like the fiction of poets concerning the wind,
I'm chiefly unruly when strongest confined.
For silver and gold I don't trouble my head,
But all I delight in is pieces of lead;
Except when I trade with a ship or a town,
Why then I make pieces of iron go down.
One property more I would have you remark,
No lady was ever more fond of a spark;
The moment I get one my soul's all a-fire,
And I roar out my joy, and in transport expire.

On a Pair of Dice

We are little brethren twain,
Arbiters of loss and gain,
Many to our counters run,
Some are made, and some undone:
But men find it to their cost,
Few are made, but numbers lost.
Though we play them tricks for ever,
Yet they always hope our favour.

On a Candle

Of all inhabitants on earth,
To man alone I owe my birth,
And yet the cow, the sheep, the bee,
Are all my parents more than he:
I, a virtue strange and rare,
Make the fairest look more fair;
And myself, which yet is rarer,
Growing old, grow still the fairer.
Like sots, alone I'm dull enough,
When dosed with smoke, and smear'd with snuff;
But in the midst of mirth and wine,
I with double lustre shine.
Emblem of the Fair am I,
Polish'd neck, and radiant eye;
In my eye my greatest grace,
Emblem of the Cyclops' race;

Metals I like them subdue,
Slave like them to Vulcan too;
Emblem of a monarch old,
Wise, and glorious to behold;
Wasted he appears, and pale,
Watching for the public weal:
Emblem of the bashful dame,
That in secret feeds her flame,
Often aiding to impart
All the secrets of her heart;
Various is my bulk and hue,
Big like Bess, and small like Sue:
Now brown and burnish'd like a nut,
At other times a very slut;
Often fair, and soft, and tender,
Taper, tall, and smooth, and slender:
Like Flora, deck'd with various flowers,
Like Phoebus, guardian of the hours:
But whatever be my dress,
Greater be my size or less,
Swelling be my shape or small,
Like thyself I shine in all.
Clouded if my face is seen,
My complexion wan and green,
Languid like a lovesick maid,
Steel affords me present aid.
Soon or late, my date is done,
As my thread of life is spun;
Yet to cut the fatal thread
Oft revives my drooping head;
Yet I perish in my prime,
Seldom by the death of time;
Die like lovers as they gaze,
Die for those I live to please;
Pine unpitied to my urn
Nor warm the fair for whom I burn;
Unpitied, unlamented too,
Die like all that look on you.

Mrs. Frances Harris's Petition

To their Excellencies the lords Justices of Ireland,
The humble petition of Frances Harris,
Who must starve and die a maid if it miscarries;
Humbly showeth, that I went to warm myself in Lady
      Betty's chamber, because I was cold;
And I had in a purse seven pounds, four shillings, and six-
      pence, besides farthings, in money and gold;
So because I had been buying things for my lady last night,
I was resolved to tell my money, to see if it was right.
Now, you must know, because my trunk has a very bad
      lock,
Therefore all the money I have, which, God knows, is a
      very small stock,
I keep in my pocket, tied about my middle, next my
      smock.
So when I went to put up my purse, as God would have it,
      my smock was unripp'd,
And instead of putting it into my pocket, down it slipp'd;
Then the bell rung, and I went down to put my lady to bed;
And, God knows, I thought my money was as safe as my
      maidenhead.
So, when I came up again, I found my pocket feel very
      light;
But when I search'd, and miss'd my purse, Lord! I thought
      I should have sunk outright.
"Lord! madam," says Mary, "how d'ye do?"—"Indeed,"
      says I, "never worse:
But pray, Mary, can you tell what I have done with my
      purse?"
"Lord help me!" says Mary, "I never stirr'd out of this
      place!"
"Nay," said I, "I had it in Lady Betty's chamber, that's a
      plain case."
So Mary got me to bed, and cover'd me up warm:
However, she stole away my garters, that I might do my-
      self no harm.
So I tumbled and toss'd all night, as you may very well
      think,
But hardly ever set my eyes together, or slept a wink.
So I was a-dream'd, methought, that I went and search'd
      the folks round,

And in a corner of Mrs. Dukes's box, tied in a rag, the
    money was found.
So next morning we told Whittle, and he fell a swearing:
Then my dame Wadger came, and she, you know, is thick
    of hearing.
"Dame," said I, as loud as I could bawl, "do you know
    what a loss I have had?"
"Nay," says she, "my Lord Colway's folks are all very sad;
For my Lord Dromedary comes a Tuesday without fail."
"Pugh!" said I, "but that's not the business that I ail."
Says Cary, says he, "I have been a servant this five and
    twenty years come spring,
And in all the places I lived I never heard of such a thing."
"Yes," says the steward, "I remember when I was at my
    Lord Shrewsbury's,
Such a thing as this happen'd, just about the time of
    gooseberries."
So I went to the party suspected, and I found her full of
    grief:
(Now, you must know, of all things in the world I hate a
    thief:)
However, I was resolved to bring the discourse slily about:
"Mrs. Dukes," said I, "here's an ugly accident has
    happened out:
'Tis not that I value the money three skips of a louse;
But the thing I stand upon is the credit of the house.
'Tis true, seven pounds, four shillings, and sixpence, makes
    a great hole in my wages:
Besides, as they say, service is no inheritance in these ages.
Now, Mrs. Dukes, you know, and everybody understands,
That though 'tis hard to judge, yet money can't go without
    hands."
"The devil take me!" said she, (blessing herself,) "if ever
    I saw't!"
So she roared like a bedlam, as though I had called her all
    to naught.
So, you know, what could I say to her any more?
I e'en left her, and came away as wise as I was before.
Well; but then they would have me gone to the cunning
    man.
"No," said I, " 'tis the same thing, the Chaplain will be
    here anon."
So the Chaplain came in. Now the servants say he is my
    sweetheart,

Because he's always in my chamber, and I always take his
    part.
So, as the devil would have it, before I was aware, out I
    blunder'd,
"Parson," said I, "can you cast a nativity, when a body's
    plunder'd?"
(Now you must know, he hates to be called Parson, like
    the devil!)
"Truly," says he, "Mrs. Nab, it might become you to be
    more civil;
If your money be gone, as a learned Divine says, d'ye see,
You are no text for my handling; so take that from me:
I was never taken for a Conjurer before, I'd have you to
    know."
"Lord!" said I, "don't be angry, I am sure I never thought
    you so;
You know I honour the cloth; I design to be a Parson's
    wife;
I never took one in your coat for a conjurer in all my life."
With that he twisted his girdle at me like a rope, as who
    should say,
"Now you may go hang yourself for me!" and so went
    away.
Well: I thought I should have swoon'd. "Lord!", said I,
    "what shall I do?
I have lost my money, and shall lose my true love too!"
Then my lord call'd me: "Harry," said my lord, "don't cry;
I'll give you something toward thy loss:" "And," says my
    lady, "so will I."
Oh! but, said I, what if, after all, the Chaplain won't come
    to?
For that, he said (an't please your Excellencies), I must
    petition you.
The premises tenderly considered, I desire your Excel-
    lencies' protection,
And that I may have a share in next Sunday's collection;
And, over and above, that I may have your Excellencies'
    letter,
With an order for the Chaplain aforesaid, or, instead of
    him, a better:
And then your poor petitioner, both night and day,
Or the Chaplain (for 'tis his trade,) as in duty bound, shall
    ever pray.

The Description of An Irish Feast

Translated almost literally out of the original Irish

O'Rourke's noble fare
    Will ne'er be forgot,
By those who were there,
    Or those who were not.

His revels to keep,
    We sup and we dine
On seven score sheep,
    Fat bullocks, and swine.

Usquebaugh to our feast
    In pails was brought up,
A hundred at least,
    And a madder our cup.

O there is the sport!
    We rise with the light
In disorderly sort,
    From snoring all night.

O how was I trick'd!
    My pipe it was broke,
My pocket was pick'd,
    I lost my new cloak.

I'm rifled, quoth Nell,
    Of mantle and kercher,
Why then fare them well,
    The de'el take the searcher.

Come, harper, strike up;
    But, first, by your favour,
Boy, give us a cup:
    Ah! this hath some savour.

O'Rourke's jolly boys
    Ne'er dreamt of the matter,
Till, roused by the noise,
    And musical clatter,

They bounce from their nest,
    No longer will tarry,
They rise ready drest,
    Without one Ave-Mary.

They dance in a round,
    Cutting capers and ramping;
A mercy the ground
    Did not burst with their stamping.

The floor is all wet
    With leaps and with jumps,
While the water and sweat
    Splish-splash in their pumps.

Bless you late and early,
    Laughlin O'Enagin!
But, my hand, you dance rarely,
    Margery Grinagin.

Bring straw for our bed,
    Shake it down to the feet,
Then over us spread
    The winnowing sheet.

To show I don't flinch,
    Fill the bowl up again:
Then give us a pinch
    Of your sneezing, a Yean.

Good Lord! what a sight,
    After all their good cheer,
For people to fight
    In the midst of their beer!

They rise from their feast,
    And hot are their brains,
A cubit at least
    The length of their skeans.

What stabs and what cuts,
    What clattering of sticks;
What strokes on the guts,
    What bastings and kicks!

With cudgels of oak,
    Well harden'd in flame,
A hundred heads broke,
    A hundred struck lame.

You churl, I'll maintain
    My father built Lusk,
The castle of Slane,
    And Carrick Drumrusk:

The Earl of Kildare,
    And Moynalta his brother,
As great as they are,
    I was nurst by their mother.

Ask that of old madam:
    She'll tell you who's who,
As far up as Adam,
    She knows it is true.

Come down with that beam,
    If cudgels are scarce,
A blow on the weam,
    Or a kick on the arse.

Baucis and Philemon

On the ever-lamented loss of the two yew-trees in the
Parish of Chilthorne, Somerset. Imitated from the Eighth
Book of Ovid.

In ancient times, as story tells,
The saints would often leave their cells,
And stroll about, but hide their quality,
To try good people's hospitality.
  It happen'd on a winter night,
As authors of the legend write,
Two brother hermits, saints by trade,
Taking their tour in masquerade,
Disguised in tatter'd habits, went
To a small village down in Kent;
Where, in the strollers' canting strain,
They begg'd from door to door in vain,
Tried every tone might pity win;
But not a soul would let them in.
  Our wandering saints, in woful state,
Treated at this ungodly rate,
Having through all the village past,
To a small cottage came at last
Where dwelt a good old honest ye'man,
Call'd in the neighbourhood Philemon;
Who kindly did these saints invite
In his poor hut to pass the night;
And then the hospitable sire
Bid Goody Baucis mend the fire;
While he from out the chimney took
A flitch of bacon off the hook,
And freely from the fattest side
Cut out large slices to be fried;
Then stepp'd aside to fetch them drink,
Fill'd a large jug up to the brink,
And saw it fairly twice go round;
Yet (what was wonderful) they found
'Twas still replenish'd to the top,
As if they ne'er had touch'd a drop.
The good old couple were amazed,
And often on each other gazed;
For both were frighten'd to the heart,

And just began to cry, "What ar't!"
Then softly turned aside, to view
Whether the lights were burning blue.
The gentle pilgrims, soon aware on't,
Told them their calling and their errand:
"Good folks, you need not be afraid,
We are but saints," the hermits said;
"No hurt shall come to you or yours:
But for that pack of churlish boors,
Not fit to live on Christian ground,
They and their houses shall be drown'd;
While you shall see your cottage rise,
And grow a church before your eyes."

  They scarce had spoke, when fair and soft,
The roof began to mount aloft;
Aloft rose every beam and rafter;
The heavy wall climb'd slowly after.

  The chimney widen'd, and grew higher,
Became a steeple with a spire.

  The kettle to the top was hoist,
And there stood fasten'd to a joist,
But with the upside down, to show
Its inclination far below:
In vain; for a superior force
Applied at bottom stops its course:
Doomed ever in suspense to dwell,
'Tis now no kettle, but a bell.

  A wooden jack, which had almost
Lost by disuse the art to roast,
A sudden alteration feels,
Increased by new intestine wheels;
And, what exalts the wonder more,
The number made the motion slower.
The flier, though it had leaden feet,
Turn'd round so quick you scarce could see't;
But, slacken'd by some secret power,
Now hardly moves an inch an hour.
The jack and chimney, near allied,
Had never left each other's side;
The chimney to a steeple grown,
The jack would not be left alone;
But, up against the steeple rear'd,
Became a clock, and still adhered;

And still it's love to household cares,
By a shrill voice at noon, declares,
Warning the cookmaid not to burn
That roast meat, which it cannot turn.

    The groaning-chair began to crawl,
Like a huge snail, along the wall;
There stuck aloft in public view,
And with small change, a pulpit grew.

    The porringers, that in a row
Hung high, and made a glittering show,
To a less noble substance changed,
Were now but leathern buckets ranged.

    The ballads, pasted on the wall,
Of Joan of France, and English Moll,
Fair Rosamond, and Robin Hood,
The little Children in the Wood,
Now seem'd to look abundance better,
Improved in picture, size and letter:
And, high in order placed, describe
The heraldry of every tribe.

    A bedstead of the antique mode,
Compact of timber many a load,
Such as our ancestors did use,
Was metamorphosed into pews;
Which still their ancient nature keep
By lodging folks disposed to sleep.

    The cottage, by such feats as these,
Grown to a church by just degrees,
The hermits then desired their host
To ask for what he fancied most.
Philemon, having paused a while,
Return'd them thanks in homely style;
Then said, "My house is grown so fine,
Methinks, I still would call it mine.
I'm old, and fain would live at ease;
Make me the parson if you please."

    He spoke, and presently he feels
His grazier's coat fall down his heels:
He sees, yet hardly can believe,
About each arm a pudding sleeve;
His waistcoat to a cassock grew,
And both assumed a sable hue;
But, being old, continued just

As threadbare, and as full of dust.
His talk was now of tithes and dues:
He smoked his pipe, and read the news;
Knew how to preach old sermons next,
Vamp'd in the preface and the text;
At christenings well could act his part,
And had the service all by heart;
Wish'd women might have children fast,
And thought whose sow had farrow'd last;
Against dissenters would repine,
And stood up firm for "right divine;"
Found his head filled with many a system;
But classic authors,—he ne'er miss'd 'em.

Thus having furbish'd up a parson,
Dame Baucis next they play'd their farce on.
Instead of homespun coifs, were seen
Good pinners edged with colberteen;
Her petticoat transform'd apace,
Became black satin, flounced with lace.
"Plain Goody" would no longer down,
'Twas "Madam," in her grogram gown.
Philemon was in great surprise,
And hardly could believe his eyes.
Amazed to see her look so prim,
And she admired as much at him.

Thus happy in their change of life,
Were several years this man and wife:
When on a day, which proved their last,
Discoursing o'er old stories past,
They went by chance, amid their talk,
To the churchyard to take a walk;
When Baucis hastily cried out,
"My dear, I see your forehead sprout!"
"Sprout," quoth the man; "what's this you tell us?
I hope you don't believe me jealous!
But yet, methinks I feel it true,
And really yours is budding too—
Nay,—now I cannot stir my foot;
It feels as if 'twere taking root."

Description would but tire my Muse,
In short, they both were turn'd to yews.
Old Goodman Dobson of the green
Remembers he the trees has seen;

He'll talk of them from noon till night,
And goes with folks to show the sight;
On Sundays, after evening prayer,
He gathers all the parish there;
Points out the place of either yew,
Here Baucis, there Philemon, grew:
Till once a parson of our town,
To mend his barn, cut Baucis down;
At which, 'tis hard to be believed
How much the other tree was grieved,
Grew scrubbed, died a-top, was stunted,
So the next parson stubb'd and burnt it.

To Stella
Who Collected and Transcribed His Poems: 1720

As, when a lofty pile is raised,
We never hear the workmen praised,
Who bring the lime, or place the stones,
But all admire Inigo Jones:
So, if this pile of scatter'd rhymes
Should be approved in aftertimes;
If it both pleases and endures,
The merit and the praise are yours.

    Thou, Stella, wert no longer young,
When first for thee my harp was strung,
Without one word of Cupid's darts,
Of killing eyes, or bleeding hearts;
With friendship and esteem possest,
I ne'er admitted Love a guest.

    In all the habitudes of life,
The friend, the mistress, and the wife,
Variety we still pursue,
In pleasure seek for something new:
Or else, comparing with the rest,
Take comfort that our own is best;
The best we value by the worst,
As tradesmen show their trash at first;
But his pursuits are at an end,
Whom Stella chooses for a friend.
A poet starving in a garret,
Conning all topics like a parrot,
Invokes his mistress and his Muse,
And stays at home for want of shoes:
Should but his Muse descending drop
A slice of bread and mutton-chop;
Or kindly, when his credit's out,
Surprise him with a pint of stout;
Or patch his broken stocking soles;
Or send him in a peck of coals;
Exalted in his mighty mind,
He flies and leaves the stars behind;
Counts all his labours amply paid,
Adores her for the timely aid.

    Or, should a porter make enquiries
For Chloe, Sylvia, Phillis, Iris;

Be told the lodging, lane, and sign,
The bowers that hold those nymphs divine;
Fair Chloe would perhaps be found
With footmen tippling underground;
The charming Sylvia beating flax,
Her shoulders mark'd with bloody tracks;
Bright Phillis mending ragged smocks:
And radiant Iris in the pox.
These are the goddesses enroll'd
In Curll's collection, new and old,
Whose scoundrel fathers would not know 'em,
If they should meet them in a poem.

    True poets can depress and raise,
Are lords of infamy and praise;
They are not scurrilous in satire,
Nor will in panegyric flatter.
Unjustly poets we asperse;
Truth shines the brighter clad in verse,
And all the fictions they pursue
Do but insinuate what is true.

    Now, should my praises owe their truth
To beauty, dress, or paint, or youth,
What stoics call without our power,
They could not be ensured an hour;
'Twere grafting on an annual stock,
That must our expectation mock,
And, making one luxuriant shoot,
Die the next year for want of root:
Before I could my verses bring,
Perhaps you're quite another thing.

    So Maevius, when he drain'd his skull
To celebrate some suburb trull,
His similes in order set,
And every crambo he could get;
Had gone through all the common-places
Worn out by wits, who rhyme on faces;
Before he could his poem close,
The lovely nymph had lost her nose.

    Your virtues safely I commend;
They on no accidents depend:
Let malice look with all her eyes,
She dares not say the poet lies.

    Stella, when you these lines transcribe,

Lest you should take them for a bribe,
Resolved to mortify your pride,
I'll here expose your weaker side.

    Your spirits kindle to a flame,
Moved by the lightest touch of blame;
And when a friend in kindness tries
To show you where your error lies,
Conviction does but more incense;
Perverseness is your whole defence;
Truth, judgment, wit, give place to spite,
Regardless of both wrong and right;
Your virtues all suspended wait,
Till time has open'd reason's gate;
And, what is worse, your passion bends
Its force against your nearest friends,
Which manners, decency, and pride,
Have taught you from the world to hide;
In vain; for see, your friend has brought
To public light your only fault;
And yet a fault we often find
Mix'd in a noble, generous mind:
And may compare to Aetna's fire,
Which, though with trembling, all admire;
The heat that makes the summit glow,
Enriching all the vales below.
Those who in warmer climes, complain
From Phoebus' rays they suffer pain,
Must own that pain is largely paid
By generous wines beneath a shade.

    Yet, when I find your passions rise,
And anger sparkling in your eyes,
I grieve those spirits should be spent,
For nobler ends by nature meant.
One passion, with a different turn,
Makes wit inflame, or anger burn:
So the sun's heat, with different powers,
Ripens the grape, the liquor sours:
Thus Ajax, when with rage possest,
By Pallas breathed into his breast,
His valour would no more employ,
Which might alone have conquer'd Troy;
But, blinded by resentment, seeks
For vengeance on his friends the Greeks.

You think this turbulence of blood
From stagnating preserves the flood,
Which, thus fermenting by degrees,
Exalts the spirits, sinks the lees.
Stella, for once you reason wrong;
For, should this ferment last too long,
By time subsiding, you may find
Nothing but acid left behind;
From passion you may then be freed,
When peevishness and spleen succeed.
Say, Stella, when you copy next,
Will you keep strictly to the text?
Dare you let these reproaches stand,
And to your failing set your hand?
Or, if these lines your anger fire,
Shall they in baser flames expire?
When'er they burn, if burn they must,
They'll prove my accusation just.

Stella's Birth-Day
1719-20

All travellers at first incline
Where'er they see the fairest sign:
And if they find the chambers neat,
And like the liquor and the meat,
Will call again, and recommend
The Angel Inn to every friend.
What though the painting grows decay'd,
The house will never lose its trade:
Nay, though the treacherous tapster, Thomas,
Hangs a new Angel two doors from us,
As fine as daubers' hands can make it,
In hopes that strangers may mistake it,
We think it both a shame and sin
To quit the true old Angel Inn   .
    Now this is Stella's case in fact,
An angel's face a little crack'd
(Could poets or could painters fix
How angels look at thirtysix:)
This drew us in at first to find
In such a form an angel's mind;
And every virtue now supplies
The fainting rays of Stella's eyes.
See at her levee crowding swains,
Whom Stella freely entertains
With breeding, humour, wit, and sense,
And puts them but to small expense;
Their mind so plentifully fills,
And makes such reasonable bills,
So little gets for what she gives,
We really wonder how she lives!
And had her stock been less, no doubt
She must have long ago run out.
    Then who can think we'll quit the place,
When Doll hangs out a newer face?
Or stop and light at Chloe's head,
With scraps and leavings to be fed?
    Then, Chloe, still go on to prate
Of thirtysix and thirtyeight;
Pursue your trade of scandal-picking,

Your hints that Stella is no chicken;
Your innuendoes, when you tell us,
That Stella loves to talk with fellows:
And let me warn you to believe
A truth, for which your soul should grieve;
That should you live to see the day,
When Stella's locks must all be gray,
When age must print a furrow'd trace
On every feature of her face;
Though you, and all your senseless tribe,
Could art, or time, or nature bribe,
To make you look like Beauty's Queen,
And hold for ever at fifteen;
No bloom of youth can ever blind
The cracks and wrinkles of your mind:
All men of sense will pass your door,
And crowd to Stella's at four-score.

To Betty, The Grisette

Queen of wit and beauty, Betty,
    Never may the Muse forget ye,
How thy face charms every shepherd,
Spotted over like a leopard!
And thy freckled neck, display'd,
Envy breeds in every maid;
Like a fly-blown cake of tallow,
Or on parchment ink turn'd yellow;
Or a tawny speckled pippin,
Shrivell'd with a winter's keeping.
    And, thy beauty thus dispatch'd,
Let me praise thy wit unmatch'd.
    Sets of phrases, cut and dry,
Evermore thy tongue supply;
And thy memory is loaded
With old scraps from plays exploded;
Stock'd with repartees and jokes,
Suited to all Christian folks:
Shreds of wit, and senseless rhymes,
Blunder'd out a thousand times;
Nor wilt thou of gifts be sparing,
Which can ne'er be worse for wearing.
Picking wit among collegians,
In the playhouse upper regions;
Where, in the eighteen-penny gallery,
Irish nymphs learn Irish raillery.
But thy merit is thy failing,
And thy raillery is railing.
    Thus with talents well endued
To be scurrilous and rude;
When you pertly raise your snout,
Fleer and gibe, and laugh and flout;
This among Hibernian asses
For sheer wit and humour passes.
Thus indulgent Chloe, bit,
Swear you have a world of wit.

My Lady's Lamentation and Complaint
Against the Dean

Sure never did man see
A wretch like poor Nancy,
So teased day and night
By a Dean and a Knight.
To punish my sins,
Sir Arthur begins,
And gives me a wipe
With Skinny and Snipe:
His malice is plain,
Hallooing the Dean.
The Dean never stops,
When he opens his chops;
I'm quite overrun
With rebus and pun.

    Before he came here,
To spunge for good cheer,
I sat with delight,
From morning till night,
With two bony thumbs
Could rub my old gums,
Or scratching my nose,
And jogging my toes;
But at present, forsooth,
I must not rub a tooth.
When my elbows he sees
Held up by my knees,
My arms, like two props,
Supporting my chops,
And just as I handle 'em
Moving all like a pendulum;
He trips up my props,
And down my chin drops,
From my head to my heels,
Like a clock without wheels;
I sink in the spleen,
A useless machine.

    If he had his will,
I should never sit still:
He comes with his whims,
I must move my limbs;

I cannot be sweet
Without using my feet;
To lengthen my breath,
He tires me to death.
By the worst of all squires,
Thro' bogs and thro' briers,
Where a cow would be startled,
I'm in spite of my heart led;
And, say what I will,
Haul'd up every hill;
Till, daggled and tatter'd,
My spirits quite shatter'd,
I return home at night,
And fast, out of spite:
For I'd rather be dead,
Than it e'er should be said,
I was better for him,
In stomach or limb.

But now to my diet;
No eating in quiet,
He's still finding fault,
Too sour or too salt:
The wing of a chick
I hardly can pick:
But trash without measure
I swallow with pleasure.

Next, for his diversion,
He rails at my person.
What court breeding this is!
He takes me to pieces:
From shoulder to flank
I'm lean and am lank;
My nose, long and thin,
Grows down to my chin;
My chin will not stay,
But meets it half way;
My fingers, prolix,
Are ten crooked sticks:
He swears my elbows
Are two iron crows,
Or sharp pointed rocks,
And wear out my smocks:
To 'scape them, Sir Arthur
Is forced to lie farther,

Or his sides they would gore
Like the tusks of a boar.
    Now changing the scene,
But still to the Dean;
He loves to be bitter at
A lady illiterate;
If he sees her but once,
He'll swear she's a dunce;
Can tell by her looks
A hater of books;
Thro' each line of her face
Her folly can trace;
Which spoils every feature
Bestow'd her by nature;
But sense gives a grace
To the homeliest face:
Wise books and reflection
Will mend the complexion:
(A civil divine!
I suppose, meaning mine!)
No lady who wants them
Can ever be handsome.
    I guess well enough
What he means by this stuff:
He haws and hums,
At last out it comes:
What, madam? No walking,
No reading, nor talking?
You're now in your prime,
Make use of your time.
Consider, before
You come to threescore,
How the hussies will fleer
Where'er you appear;
"That silly old puss
Would fain be like us:
What a figure she made
In her tarnish'd brocade!"
    And then he grows mild:
Come, be a good child:
If you are inclined
To polish your mind,
Be adored by the men
Till threescore and ten,

And kill with the spleen
The jades of sixteen;
I'll show you the way;
Read six hours a-day.
The wits will frequent ye,
And think you but twenty.
(To make you learn faster,
I'll be your schoolmaster,
And leave you to choose
The books you peruse.)
    Thus was I drawn in;
Forgive me my sin.
At breakfast he'll ask
An account of my task.
Put a word out of joint,
Or miss but a point,
He rages and frets,
His manners forgets;
And as I am serious,
Is very imperious.
No book for delight
Must come in my sight;
But, instead of new plays,
Dull Bacon's Essays,
And pore every day on
That nasty Pantheon.
If I be not a drudge,
Let all the world judge.
'Twere better be blind,
Than thus be confined.
    But while in an ill tone
I murder poor Milton,
The Dean you will swear,
Is at study or prayer.
He's all the day sauntering,
With labourers bantering,
Among his colleagues,
A parcel of Teagues,
Whom he brings in among us
And bribes with mundungus.
(He little believes
How they laugh in their sleeves.)
Hail, fellow, well met,
All dirty and wet:

Find out, if you can,
Who's master, who's man;
Who makes the best figure,
The Dean or the digger;
And which is the best
At cracking a jest.
(Now see how he sits
Perplexing his wits
In search of a motto
To fix on his grotto.)
How proudly he talks
Of zigzags and walks,
And all the day raves
Of cradles and caves;
And boasts of his feats,
His grottos and seats;
Shows all his gewgaws,
And gapes for applause;
A fine occupation
For one in his station!
A hole where a rabbit
Would scorn to inhabit,
Dug out in an hour;
He calls it a bower.

But, O! how we laugh,
To see a wild calf
Come, driven by heat,
And foul the green seat;
Or run helter-skelter,
To his arbour for shelter,
Where all goes to ruin
The Dean has been doing:
The girls of the village
Come flocking for pillage,
Pull down the fine briers
And thorns to make fires;
But yet are so kind
To leave something behind:
No more need be said on't,
I smell when I tread on't.

Dear friend, Doctor Jinny,
If I could but win ye,
Or Walmsley, or Whaley,
To come hither daily,

Since fortune, my foe,
Will needs have it so,
That I'm, by her frowns,
Condemn'd to black gowns;
No squire to be found
The neighbourhood round;
(For, under the rose,
I would rather choose those)
If your wives will permit ye,
Come here out of pity,
To ease a poor lady,
And beg her a play-day.
So may you be seen
No more in the spleen;
May Walmsley give wine
Like a hearty divine!
May Whaley disgrace
Dull Daniel's whey-face!
And may your three spouses
Let you lie at friends' houses!

A Panegyric on the Dean
In the Person of a Lady in the North

Resolved my gratitude to show,
Thrice reverend Dean, for all I owe,
Too long I have my thanks delay'd;
Your favours left too long unpaid;
But now, in all our sex's name,
My artless Muse shall sing your fame.
    Indulgent you to female kind,
To all their weaker sides are blind;
Nine more such champions as the Dean
Would soon restore our ancient reign;
How well to win the ladies' hearts,
You celebrate their wit and parts!
How have I felt my spirits raised,
By you so oft, so highly praised!
Transform'd by your convincing tongue
To witty, beautiful, and young,
I hope to quit that awkward shame,
Affected by each vulgar dame,
To modesty a weak pretence;
And soon grow pert on men of sense;
To show my face with scornful air;
Let others match it if they dare.
    Impatient to be out of debt,
O, may I never once forget
The bard who humbly deigns to choose
Me for the subject of his Muse!
Behind my back, before my nose,
He sounds my praise in verse and prose.
    My heart with emulation burns,
To make you suitable returns;
My gratitude the world shall know;
And see, the printer's boy below;
Ye hawkers all, your voices lift;
"A Panegyric on Dean Swift!"
And then, to mend the matter still,
"By Lady Anne of Market-Hill!"
    I thus begin: My grateful Muse
Salutes the Dean in different views;
Dean, butler, usher, jester, tutor;
Robert and Darby's coadjutor;
And, as you in commission sit,

To rule the diary next to Kit;
In each capacity I mean
To sing your praise. And first as Dean:
Envy must own you understand your
Precedence, and support your grandeur:
Nor of your rank will bate an ace,
Except to give Dean Daniel place.
In you such dignity appears,
So suited to your state and years!
With ladies what a strict decorum!
With what devotion you adore 'em!
Treat me with so much complaisance,
As fits a princess in romance!
By your example and assistance,
The fellows learn to know their distance.
Sir Arthur, since you set the pattern,
No longer calls me snipe and slattern,
Nor dares he, though he were a duke,
Offend me with the least rebuke.

    Proceed we to your preaching next!
How nice you split the hardest text!
How your superior learning shines
Above our neighbouring dull divines!
At Beggar's Opera not so full pit
Is seen as when you mount our pulpit.

    Consider now your conversation:
Regardful of your age and station,
You ne'er were known by passion stirr'd,
To give the least offensive word:
But still, whene'er you silence break,
Watch every syllable you speak:
Your style so clear and so concise,
We never ask to hear you twice.
But then a parson so genteel,
So nicely clad from head to heel;
So fine a gown, a band so clean,
As well become St. Patrick's dean,
Such reverential awe express,
That cowboys know you by your dress!
Then, if our neighbouring friends come here,
How proud are we when you appear,
With such address and graceful port,
As clearly shows you bred at court!

    Now raise your spirits, Mr. Dean,

I lead you to a nobler scene.
When to the vault you walk in state,
In quality of butler's mate;
You next to Dennis bear the sway:
To you we often trust the key:
Nor can he judge with all his art
So well what bottle holds a quart:
What pints may best for bottles pass,
Just to give every man his glass:
When proper to produce the best;
And what may serve a common guest.
With Dennis you did ne'er combine,
Not you, to steal your master's wine;
Except a bottle now and then,
To welcome brother serving-men;
But that is with a good design,
To drink Sir Arthur's health and mine:
Your master's honour to maintain:
And get the like returns again.

    Your usher's post must next be handled:
How blest am I by such a man led!
Under whose wise and careful guardship
I now despise fatigue and hardship;
Familiar grown to dirt and wet,
Though draggled round, I scorn to fret:
From you my chamber damsels learn
My broken hose to patch and darn.

    Now as a jester I accost you;
Which never yet one friend has lost you.
You judge so nicely to a hair,
How far to go, and when to spare;
By long experience grown so wise,
Of every taste to know the size;
There's none so ignorant or weak
To take offence at what you speak.
Whene'er you joke, 'tis all a case
Whether with Dermot or his grace;
With Teague O'Murphy, or an earl;
A duchess, or a kitchen girl.
With such dexterity you fit
Their several talents with your wit,
That Moll the chambermaid can smoke,
And Gahagan take every joke.

    I now become your humble suitor

To let me praise you as my tutor.
Poor I, a savage bred and born,
By you instructed every morn,
Already have improved so well,
That I have almost learnt to spell:
The neighbours who come here to dine,
Admire to hear me speak so fine.
How enviously the ladies look,
When they surprise me at my book!
And sure as they're alive at night,
As soon as gone will show their spite:
Good lord! what can my lady mean,
Conversing with that rusty Dean?
She's grown so nice, and so penurious,
With Socrates and Epicurius!
How could she sit the livelong day,
Yet never ask us once to play?

But I admire your patience most;
That when I'm duller than a post,
Nor can the plainest word pronounce,
You neither fume, nor fret, nor flounce;
Are so indulgent, and so mild,
As if I were a darling child.
So gentle is your whole proceeding,
That I could spend my life in reading.

You merit new employments daily:
Our thatcher, ditcher, gardener, baily.
And to a genius so extensive
No work is grievous or offensive:
Whether your fruitful fancy lies
To make for pigs convenient styes;
Or ponder long with anxious thought
To banish rats that haunt our vault:
Nor have you grumbled, reverend Dean,
To keep our poultry sweet and clean;
To sweep the mansion-house they dwell in,
And cure the rank unsavoury smelling.

Now enter as the dairy handmaid:
Such charming butter never man made.
Let others with fanatic face
Talk of their milk for babes of grace;
From tubs their snuffling nonsense utter;
Thy milk shall make us tubs of butter.
The bishop with his foot may burn it,

But with his hand the Dean can churn it.
How are the servants overjoy'd
To see thy deanship thus employ'd!
Instead of poring on a book,
Providing butter for the cook!
Three morning hours you toss and shake
The bottle till your fingers ache;
Hard is the toil, nor small the art,
The butter from the whey to part:
Behold a frothy substance rise;
Be cautious or your bottle flies.
The butter comes, our fears are ceas'd;
And out you squeeze an ounce at least.

    Your reverence thus with like success,
(Nor is your skill or labour less,)
When bent upon some smart lampoon,
Will toss and turn your brain till noon;
Which in its jumblings round the skull,
Dilates and makes the vessel full:
While nothing comes but froth at first,
You think your giddy head will burst;
But squeezing out four lines in rhyme,
Are largely paid for all your time.

    But you have raised your generous mind
To works of more exalted kind.
Palladio was not half so skill'd in
The grandeur or the art of building.
Two temples of magnific size
Attract the curious traveller's eyes,
That might be envied by the Greeks;
Raised up by you in twenty weeks:
Here gentle goddess Cloacine
Receives all offerings at her shrine.
In separate cells the he's and she's,
Here pay their vows on bended knees:
For 'tis profane when sexes mingle,
And every nymph must enter single;
And when she feels an inward motion,
Come fill'd with reverence and devotion.
The bashful maid, to hide her blush,
Shall creep no more behind a bush;
Here unobserved she boldly goes,
As who should say, to pluck a rose.

    Ye, who frequent this hallow'd scene,

Be not ungrateful to the Dean;
But duly, ere you leave your station,
Offer to him a pure libation,
Or of his own or Smedley's lay,
Or billet-doux, or lock of hay:
And, O! may all who hither come,
Return with unpolluted thumb!

  Yet, when your lofty domes I praise,
I sigh to think of ancient days.
Permit me then to raise my style,
And sweetly moralize a-while.

  Thee, bounteous goddess Cloacine,
To temples why do we confine?
Forbid in open air to breathe,
Why are thine altars fix'd beneath?
When Saturn ruled the skies alone,
(That golden age to gold unknown,)
This earthly globe, to thee assign'd,
Received the gifts of all mankind.
Ten thousand altars smoking round,
Were built to thee with offerings crown'd;
And here thy daily votaries placed
Their sacrifice with zeal and haste:
The margin of a purling stream
Sent up to thee a grateful steam;
Though sometimes thou wert pleased to wink,
If Naiads swept them from the brink:
Or where appointing lovers rove,
The shelter of a shady grove;
Or offer'd in some flowery vale,
Were wafted by a gentle gale,
There many a flower abstersive grew,
Thy favourite flowers of yellow hue;
The crocus and the daffodil,
The cowslip soft, and sweet jonquil.

  But when at last usurping Jove
Old Saturn from his empire drove,
Then gluttony, with greasy paws,
Her napkin pinn'd up to her jaws,
With watery chops, and wagging chin,
Braced like a drum her oily skin;
Wedged in a spacious elbow-chair,
And on her plate a treble share,
As if she ne'er could have enough,

Taught harmless man to cram and stuff.
She sent her priests in wooden shoes
From haughty Gaul to make ragous;
Instead of wholesome bread and cheese,
To dress their soups and fricassees;
And, for our home-bred British cheer,
Botargo, catsup, and caveer.

This bloated harpy, sprung from hell,
Confined thee, goddess, to a cell:
Sprung from her womb that impious line,
Contemners of thy rites divine.
First, lolling Sloth in woolen cap,
Taking her after-dinner nap:
Pale Dropsy, with a sallow face,
Her belly burst, and slow her pace:
And lordly Gout, wrapt up in fur,
And wheezing Asthma, loth to stir:
Voluptuous Ease, the child of wealth,
Infecting thus our hearts by stealth.
None seek thee now in open air,
To thee no verdant altars rear;
But, in their cells and vaults obscene,
Present a sacrifice unclean;
From whence unsavoury vapours rose,
Offensive to thy nicer nose.
Ah! who in our degenerate days,
As nature prompts, his offering pays?
Here nature never difference made
Between the sceptre and the spade.

Ye great ones, why will ye disdain
To pay your tribute on the plain?
Why will you place in lazy pride
Your altars near your couches' side;
When from the homeliest earthen ware
Are sent up offerings more sincere,
Than where the haughty duchess locks
Her silver vase in cedar box?

Yet some devotion still remains
Among our harmless northern swains,
Whose offerings, placed in golden ranks,
Adorn our crystal rivers' banks;
Nor seldom grace the flowery downs,
With spiral tops and copple crowns;
Or gilding in a sunny morn

The humble branches of a thorn.
So poets sing, with golden bough
The Trojan hero paid his vow.

    Hither, by luckless error led,
The crude consistence oft I tread;
Here when my shoes are out of case,
Unweeting gild the tarnish'd lace;
Here, by the sacred bramble tinged,
My petticoat is doubly fringed.

    Be witness for me, nymph divine,
I never robb'd thee with design;
Nor will the zealous Hannah pout
To wash thy injured offering out.
But stop, ambitious Muse, in time,
Nor dwell on subjects too sublime.
In vain on lofty heels I tread,
Aspiring to exalt my head;
With hoop expanded wide and light,
In vain I 'tempt too high a flight.

    Me Phoebus in a midnight dream
Accosting, said, "Go shake your cream.
Be humbly-minded, know your post;
Sweeten your tea, and watch your toast.
Thee best befits a lowly style;
Teach Dennis how to stir the guile;
With Peggy Dixon thoughtful sit,
Contriving for the pot and spit.
Take down thy proudly swelling sails,
And rub thy teeth and pare thy nails;
At nicely carving show thy wit;
But ne'er presume to eat a bit:
Turn every way thy watchful eye,
And every guest be sure to ply:
Let never at your board be known
An empty plate, except your own.
Be these thy arts; nor higher aim
Than what befits a rural dame.

    "But Cloacina, goddess bright,
Sleek————claims her as his right;
And Smedley, flower of all divines,
Shall sing the Dean in Smedley's lines."

Addressed to the Earl of Oxford,
Prime Minister of England

Harley, the nation's great support,
Returning home one day from court,
(His mind with public cares possest,
All Europe's business in his breast,)
Observed a parson near Whitehall,
Cheapening old authors on a stall.
The priest was pretty well in case,
And show'd some humour in his face;
Look'd with an easy, careless mien,
A perfect stranger to the spleen;
Of size that might a pulpit fill,
But more inclining to sit still.
My lord (who, if a man may say't,
Loves mischief better than his meat)
Was now disposed to crack a jest,
And bid friend Lewis go in quest
(This Lewis is a cunning shaver,
And very much in Harley's favour)—
In quest who might this parson be,
What was his name, of what degree;
If possible, to learn his story,
And whether he were Whig or Tory.
        Lewis his patron's humour knows,
Away upon his errand goes,
And quickly did the matter sift;
Found out that it was Doctor Swift;
A clergyman of special note
For shunning those of his own coat;
Which made his brethren of the gown
Take care betimes to run him down:
No libertine, nor over nice,
Addicted to no sort of vice,
Went where he pleased, said what he thought;
Not rich, but owed no man a groat,
In state opinions a la mode,
He hated Wharton like a toad,
Had given the faction many a wound,
And libell'd all the junto round;
Kept company with men of wit,
Who often father'd what he writ:

His works were hawk'd in every street,
But seldom rose above a sheet:
Of late, indeed, the paper stamp
Did very much his genius cramp;
And, since he could not spend his fire,
He now intended to retire.

Said Harley, "I desire to know
From his own mouth, if this be so;
Step to the doctor straight, and say,
I'd have him dine with me to-day."
Swift seem'd to wonder what he meant,
Nor would believe my lord had sent;
So never offer'd once to stir,
But coldly said, "Your servant, sir!"
"Does he refuse me?" Harley cried:
"He does, with insolence and pride."

Some few days after, Harley spies
The doctor fasten'd by the eyes
At Charing-cross, among the rout,
Where painted monsters are hung out:
He pull'd the string, and stopt his coach,
Beckoning the doctor to approach.
Swift, who could neither fly nor hide,
Came sneaking to the chariot side,
And offer'd many a lame excuse:
He never meant the least abuse—
"My lord—the honour you design'd—
Extremely proud—but I had dined—
I'm sure I never should neglect—
No man alive has more respect"—
"Well, I shall think of that no more,
If you'll be sure to come at four."

The doctor now obeys the summons,
Likes both his company and commons;
Displays his talents, sits till ten;
Next day invited, comes again;
Soon grows domestic, seldom fails
Either at morning or at meals;
Came early and departed late;
In short, the gudgeon took the bait.
My lord would carry on the jest,
And down to Windsor takes his guest.
Swift much admires the place and air,
And longs to be a canon there;

In summer round the Park to ride,
In winter—never to reside.
A canon!—that's a place too mean:
No, doctor, you shall be a dean;
Two dozen canons round your stall,
And you the tyrant o'er them all:
You need but cross the Irish seas,
To live in plenty, power, and ease.
Poor Swift departs, and, what is worse,
With borrow'd money in his purse,
Travels at least a hundred leagues,
And suffers numberless fatigues.

    Suppose him now a dean complete,
Demurely lolling in his seat:
The silver verge, with decent pride,
Stuck underneath his cushion side;
Suppose him gone through all vexations,
Patents, instalments, abjurations,
First-fruits, and tenths, and chapter-treats;
Dues, payments, fees, demands, and cheats—
The wicked laity's contriving
To hinder clergymen from thriving.
Now, all the doctor's money spent,
His tenants wrong him in his rent;
The farmers, spitefully combined,
Force him to take his tithes in kind,
And Parvisol discounts arrears
By bills for taxes and repairs.

    Poor Swift, with all his losses vex'd,
Not knowing where to turn him next,
Above a thousand pounds in debt,
Takes horse, and in a mighty fret
Rides day and night at such a rate,
He soon arrives at Harley's gate;
But was so dirty, pale, and thin,
Old Read would hardly let him in.

    Said Harley, "Welcome, reverend dean!
What makes your worship look so lean?
Why, sure you won't appear in town
In that old wig and rusty gown?
I doubt your heart is set on pelf
So much that you neglect yourself.
What! I suppose, now stocks are high,
You've some good purchase in your eye?

Or is your money out at use?"—
    "Truce, good my lord, I beg a truce,"
(The doctor in a passion cried,)
"Your raillery is misapplied;
Experience I have dearly bought;
You know I am not worth a groat:
But you resolved to have your jest,
And 'twas a folly to contest;
Then, since you now have done your worst,
Pray leave me where you found me first."

On the Death of Dr. Swift

Written in November 1731

As Rochefacault his maxims drew
From nature, I believe them true;
They argue no corrupted mind
In him; the fault is in mankind.
    This maxim more than all the rest
Is thought too base for human breast:
"In all distresses of our friends,
We first consult our private ends;
While nature, kindly bent to ease us,
Points out some circumstance to please us."
    If this perhaps your patience move,
Let reason and experience prove.
We all behold with envious eyes
Our equals raised above our size.
Who would not at a crowded show
Stand high himself, keep others low?
I love my friend as well as you:
But why should he obstruct my view?
Then let me have the higher post:
Suppose it but an inch at most.
If in a battle you should find
One whom you love of all mankind,
Had some heroic action done,
A champion kill'd, or trophy won;
Rather than thus be overtopp'd,
Would you not wish his laurels cropp'd?
Dear honest Ned is in the gout,
Lies rack'd with pain, and you without:
How patiently you hear him groan!
How glad the case is not your own!
    What poet would not grieve to see
His brethren write as well as he?
But rather than they should excel,
He'd wish his rivals all in hell?
    Her end when Emulation misses,
She turns to Envy, stings, and hisses:
The strongest friendship yields to pride,
Unless the odds be on our side.
Vain human kind! fantastic race!

Thy various follies who can trace?
Self-love, ambition, envy, pride,
Their empire in our hearts divide.
Give others riches, power and station,
'Tis all on me a usurpation.
I have no title to aspire;
Yet, when you sink, I seem the higher.
In Pope I cannot read a line,
But with a sigh I wish it mine;
When he can in one couplet fix
More sense than I can do in six;
It gives me such a jealous fit,
I cry, "Pox take him and his wit!"
I grieve to be outdone by Gay
In my own humorous biting way.
Arbuthnot is no more my friend,
Who dares to irony pretend,
Which I was born to introduce,
Refined it first, and showed its use.
St. John, as well as Pultney, knows
That I had some repute for prose;
And, till they drove me out of date,
Could maul a minister of state.
If they have mortified my pride,
And made me throw my pen aside;
If with such talents Heaven has bless'd 'em,
Have I not reason to detest 'em?
　　　To all my foes, dear Fortune, send
Thy gifts; but never to my friend:
I tamely can endure the first;
But this with envy makes me burst.
　　　Thus much may serve my way of proem:
Proceed we therefore to our poem.
　　　The time is not remote, when I
Must by the course of nature, die;
When, I foresee, my special friends
Will try to find their private ends:
And, though 'tis hardly understood
Which way my death can do them good,
Yet thus, methinks, I hear them speak:
"See, how the Dean begins to break!
Poor gentleman, he droops apace!
You plainly find it in his face.
That old vertigo in his head

Will never leave him till he's dead.
Besides, his memory decays:
He recollects not what he says;
He cannot call his friends to mind;
Forgets the place where last he dined;
Plies you with stories o'er and o'er;
He told them fifty times before.
How does he fancy we can sit
To hear his out-of-fashion wit?
But he takes up with younger folks,
Who for his wine will bear his jokes.
Faith! he must make his stories shorter,
Or change his comrades once a quarter:
In half the time he talks them round,
There must another set be found.

    "For poetry he's past his prime:
He takes an hour to find a rhyme;
His fire is out, his wit decay'd,
His fancy sunk, his Muse a jade.
I'd have him throw away his pen;—
But there's no talking to some men!"

    And then their tenderness appears,
By adding largely to my years;
"He's older than he would be reckon'd,
And well remembers Charles the Second.
He hardly drinks a pint of wine;
And that, I doubt, is no good sign.
His stomach, too, begins to fail:
Last year we thought him strong and hale;
But now he's quite another thing:
I wish he may hold out till spring!"
They hug themselves, and reason thus:
"It is not yet so bad with us!"

    In such a case, they talk in tropes,
And by their fears express their hopes.
Some great misfortune to portend,
No enemy can match a friend.
With all the kindness they profess,
The merit of a lucky guess
(When daily how d'y's come of course,
And servants answer, "Worse and worse!")
Would please them better, than to tell,
That, "God be praised, the Dean is well."
Then he, who prophesied the best,

Approves his foresight to the rest:
"You know I always fear'd the worst,
And often told you so at first."
He'd rather choose that I should die,
Than his prediction prove a lie.
Not one foretells I shall recover;
But all agree to give me over.

    Yet, should some neighbour feel a pain
Just in the parts where I complain;
How many a message would he send!
What hearty prayers that I should mend!
Inquire what regimen I kept;
What gave me ease, and how I slept?
And more lament when I was dead,
Than all the snivellers round my bed.

    My good companions, never fear;
For though you may mistake a year,
Though your prognostics run too fast,
They must be verified at last.

    Behold the fatal day arrive!
"How is the Dean?"—"He's just alive."
Now the departing prayer is read;
"He hardly breathes."—"The Dean is dead."

    Before the passing bell begun,
The news through half the town is run.
"O! may we all for death prepare!
What has he left? and who's his heir?"—
"I know no more than what the news is;
'Tis all bequeath'd to public uses."—
"To public uses! a perfect whim!
What had the public done for him?
Mere envy, avarice, and pride:
He gave it all—but first he died.
And had the Dean, in all the nation,
No worthy friend, no poor relation?
So ready to do strangers good,
Forgetting his own flesh and blood?"

    Now, Grub-Street wits are all employ'd;
With elegies the town is cloy'd:
Some paragraph in every paper
To curse the Dean, or bless the Drapier.

    The doctors, tender of their fame,
Wisely on me lay all the blame:
"We must confess, his case was nice;

But he would never take advice.
Had he been ruled, for aught appears,
He might have lived these twenty years;
For, when we open'd him, we found,
That all his vital parts were sound."

From Dublin soon to London spread,
'Tis told at court, "The Dean is dead."
Kind Lady Suffolk, in the spleen,
Runs laughing up to tell the queen.
The queen, so gracious, mild, and good,
Cries, "Is he gone! 'tis time he should.
He's dead, you say; then let him rot:
I'm glad the medals were forgot.
I promis'd him, I own; but when?
I only was the princess then;
But now, as consort of the king,
You know, 'tis quite another thing."
Now Chartres, at Sir Robert's levee,
Tells with a sneer the tidings heavy:
"Why, if he died without his shoes,"
Cries Bob, "I'm sorry for the news:
O, were the wretch but living still,
And in his place my good friend Will!
Or had a mitre on his head,
Provided Bolingbroke were dead!"
Now Curll his shop from rubbish drains:
Three genuine tomes of Swift's remains!
And then, to make them pass the glibber,
Revised by Tibbalds, Moore, and Cibber.
He'll treat me as he does my betters,
Publish my will, my life, my letters.
Revive the libels born to die;
Which Pope must bear, as well as I.

Here shift the scene, to represent
How those I love my death lament.
Poor Pope would grieve a month, and Gay
A week, and Arbuthnot a day.

St. John himself will scarce forbear
To bite his pen, and drop a tear.
The rest will give a shrug, and cry,
"I'm sorry—but we all must die!"

Indifference, clad in Wisdom's guise,
All fortitude of mind supplies:
For how can stony bowels melt

In those who never pity felt!
When we are lash'd, they kiss the rod,
Resigning to the will of God.

The fools, my juniors by a year,
Are tortur'd with suspense and fear;
Who wisely thought my age a screen,
When death approach'd, to stand between:
The screen removed, their hearts are trembling;
They mourn for me without dissembling.

My female friends, whose tender hearts
Have better learn'd to act their parts,
Receive the news in doleful dumps:
"The Dean is dead: (Pray what is trumps?)
Then, Lord have mercy on his soul!
(Ladies, I'll venture for the vole.)
Six deans, they say, must bear the pall:
(I wish I knew what king to call.)
Madam, your husband will attend
The funeral of so good a friend.
No, madam, 'tis a shocking sight:
And he's engaged tomorrow night:
My Lady Club will take it ill,
If he should fail her at quadrille.
He loved the Dean—(I led a heart,)
But dearest friends, they say, must part.
His time was come: he ran his race;
We hope he's in a better place."

Why do we grieve that friends should die?
No loss more easy to supply.
One year is past; a different scene!
No further mention of the Dean;
Who now, alas! no more is miss'd,
Than if he never did exist.
Where's now this favourite of Apollo!
Departed:—and his works must follow;
Must undergo the common fate;
His kind of wit is out of date.

Some country squire to Lintot goes,
Inquires for "Swift in Verse and Prose."
Says Lintot, "I have heard the name;
He died a year ago." "The same."
He searches all the shop in vain.
"Sir, you may find them in Duck-lane;
I sent them with a load of books,

Last Monday to the pastry-cook's.
To fancy they could live a year!
I find you're but a stranger here.
The Dean was famous in his time,
And had a kind of knack at rhyme.
His way of writing now is past;
The town has got a better taste;
I keep no antiquated stuff,
But spick and span I have enough.
Pray do but give me leave to show 'em
Here's Colley Cibber's birth-day poem.
This ode you never yet have seen,
By Stephen Duck, upon the queen.
Then here's a letter, finely penn'd
Against the Craftsman and his friend;
It clearly shows that all reflection
On ministers is disaffection.
Next, here's Sir Robert's vindication,
And Mr. Henley's last oration.
The hawkers have not got them yet;
Your honour please to buy a set?

    "Here's Wolston's tracts, the twelfth edition;
'Tis read by every politician;
The country members, when in town,
To all their boroughs send them down;
You never met a thing so smart;
The courtiers have them all by heart:
Those maids of honour who can read,
Are taught to use them for their creed.
The reverend author's good intention
Has been rewarded with a pension.
He does an honour to his gown,
By bravely running priestcraft down:
He shows, as sure as God's in Gloucester,
That Moses was a grand impostor;
That all his miracles were cheats,
Perform'd as jugglers do their feats:
The church had never such a writer;
A shame he has not got a mitre!"

    Suppose me dead; and then suppose
A club assembled at the Rose;
Where, from discourse of this and that,
I grow the subject of their chat.
And while they toss my name about,

With favour some, and some without,
One, quite indifferent in the cause,
My character impartial draws:
        "The Dean, if we believe report,
Was never ill-received at court.
As for his works in verse and prose,
I own myself no judge of those:
Nor can I tell what critics thought 'em:
But this I know, all people bought 'em.
As with a moral view design'd
To cure the vices of mankind:
His vein, ironically grave,
Expos'd the fool, and lash'd the knave.
To steal a hint was never known,
But what he writ was all his own.
        "He never thought an honour done him,
Because a duke was proud to own him;
Would rather slip aside and choose
To talk with wits in dirty shoes;
Despised the fools with stars and garters,
So often seen caressing Chartres.
He never courted men in station,
Nor persons held in admiration;
Of no man's greatness was afraid,
Because he sought for no man's aid.
Though trusted long in great affairs,
He gave himself no haughty airs:
Without regarding private ends,
Spent all his credit for his friends;
And only chose the wise and good;
No flatterers; no allies in blood;
But succour'd virtue in distress,
And seldom fail'd of good success;
As numbers in their hearts must own,
Who, but for him, had been unknown.
        "With princes kept a due decorum,
But never stood in awe before 'em.
He follow'd David's lesson just;
In princes never put thy trust:
And would you make him truly sour,
Provoke him with a slave in power.
The Irish senate if you named,
With what impatience he declaim'd!
Fair LIBERTY was all his cry,

For her he stood prepared to die;
For her he boldly stood alone;
For her he oft exposed his own.
Two kingdoms, just as faction led,
Had set a price upon his head;
But not a traitor could be found,
To sell him for six hundred pound.

    "Had he but spared his tongue and pen,
He might have rose like other men:
But power was never in his thought,
And wealth he valued not a groat:
Ingratitude he often found,
And pitied those who meant the wound:
But kept the tenor of his mind,
To merit well of human kind:
Nor made a sacrifice of those
Who still were true, to please his foes.
He labour'd many a fruitless hour,
To reconcile his friends in power;
Saw mischief by a faction brewing,
While they pursued each other's ruin.
But finding vain was all his care,
He left the court in mere despair.

    "And, oh! how short are human schemes!
Here ended all our golden dreams.
What St. John's skill in state affairs,
What Ormond's valour, Oxford's cares,
To save their sinking country lent,
Was all destroy'd by one event.
Too soon that precious life was ended,
On which alone our weal depended.
When up a dangerous faction starts,
With wrath and vengeance in their hearts;
By solemn league and covenant bound,
To ruin, slaughter, and confound;
To turn religion to a fable,
And make the government a Babel;
Pervert the laws, disgrace the gown,
Corrupt the senate, rob the crown;
To sacrifice old England's glory,
And make her infamous in story:
When such a tempest shook the land,
How could unguarded Virtue stand!
With horror, grief, despair, the Dean

Beheld the dire, destructive scene:
His friends in exile, or the tower,
Himself within the frown of power;
Pursued by base envenom'd pens,
Far to the land of saints and fens;
A servile race in folly nursed,
Who truckle most, when treated worst.

"By innocence and resolution,
He bore continual persecution,
While numbers to preferment rose,
Whose merits were, to be his foes;
When e'en his own familiar friends,
Intent upon their private ends,
Like renegadoes now he feels,
Against him lifting up their heels.

"The Dean did, by his pen, defeat
An infamous destructive cheat;
Taught fools their interest how to know,
And gave them arms to ward the blow.
Envy has own'd it was his doing,
To save that hapless land from ruin;
While they who at the steerage stood,
And reap'd the profit, sought his blood.

"To save them from their evil fate,
In him was held a crime of state.
A wicked monster on the bench,
Whose fury blood could never quench;
As vile and profligate a villain,
As modern Scroggs, or old Tresilian:
Who long all justice has discarded,
Nor fear'd he God, nor man regarded;
Vow'd on the Dean his rage to vent,
And make him of his zeal repent:
But Heaven his innocence defends,
The grateful people stand his friends;
Not strains of law, nor judge's frown,
Nor topics brought to please the crown,
Nor witness hired, nor jury pick'd,
Prevail to bring him in convict.

"In exile, with a steady heart,
He spent his life's declining part;
Where folly, pride, and faction sway,
Remote from St. John, Pope and Gay.
His friendships there, to few confin'd,

Were always of the middling kind;
No fools of rank, a mongrel breed,
Who fain would pass for lords indeed:
Where titles give no right to power,
And peerage is a wither'd flower;
He would have held it a disgrace,
If such a wretch had known his face.
On rural squires, that kingdom's bane,
He vented oft his wrath in vain;
Biennial squires to market brought;
Who sell their souls and votes for nought.
The country stript, go joyful back,
To rob the church, their tenants rack,
Go snacks with thieves and rapparees
And keep the peace to pick up fees;
In every job to have a share,
A gaol or turnpike to repair;
And turn the tax for public roads,
Commodious to their own abodes.

    "Perhaps I may allow the Dean
Had too much satire in his vein;
And seem'd determined not to starve it,
Because no age could more deserve it.
Yet malice never was his aim;
He lash'd the vice, but spared the name;
No individual could resent,
Where thousands equally were meant;
His satire points at no defect,
But what all mortals may correct;
For he abhorr'd that senseless tribe
Who call it humour when they gibe:
He spared a hump, or crooked nose,
Whose owners set not up for beaux.
True genuine dulness moved his pity,
Unless it offer'd to be witty.
Those who their ignorance confest,
He ne'er offended with a jest;
But laugh'd to hear an idiot quote
A verse from Horace learn'd by rote.

    "He knew a hundred pleasing stories,
With all the turns of Whigs and Tories:
Was cheerful to his dying day;
And friends would let him have his way.

    "He gave the little wealth he had

To build a house for fools and mad;
And show'd by one satiric touch,
No nation wanted it so much.
That kingdom he had left his debtor,
I wish it soon may have a better."

Stella to Dr. Swift

On his Birth-day, Nov. 30, 1721

St. Patrick's Dean, your country's pride,
My early and my only guide,
Let me among the rest attend,
Your pupil and your humble friend,
To celebrate in female strains
The day that paid your mother's pains;
Descend to take that tribute due
In gratitude alone to you.

  When men began to call me fair,
You interposed your timely care:
You early taught me to despise
The ogling of a coxcomb's eyes;
Show'd where my judgment was misplac'd;
Refined my fancy and my taste.

  Behold that beauty just decay'd,
Invoking art to nature's aid:
Forsook by her admiring train,
She spreads her tatter'd nets in vain;
Short was her part upon the stage;
Went smoothly on for half a page;
Her bloom was gone, she wanted art,
As the scene changed, to change her part;
She, whom no lover could resist,
Before the second act was hiss'd.
Such is the fate of female race
With no endowments but a face;
Before the thirtieth year of life,
A maid forlorn, or hated wife.

  Stella to you, her tutor, owes
That she has ne'er resembled those:
Nor was a burden to mankind
With half her course of years behind.
You taught how I might youth prolong,
By knowing what was right and wrong;
How from my heart to bring supplies
Of lustre to my fading eyes;
How soon a beauteous mind repairs
The loss of changed or falling hairs;
How wit and virtue from within
Send out a smoothness o'er the skin:

Your lectures could my fancy fix,
And I can please at thirtysix.
The sight of Chloe at fifteen,
Coquetting, gives me not the spleen;
The idol now of every fool
Till time shall make their passions cool;
Then tumbling down Time's steepy hill,
While Stella holds her station still.
O! turn your precepts into laws,
Redeem the women's ruin'd cause,
Retrieve lost empire to our sex,
That men may bow their rebel necks.

      Long be the day that gave you birth
Sacred to friendship, wit, and mirth;
Late dying may you cast a shred
Of your rich mantle o'er my head;
To bear with dignity my sorrow,
One day alone, then die tomorrow.

Cadenus and Vanessa

The shepherds and the nymphs were seen
Pleading before the Cyprian queen.
The counsel for the fair began,
Accusing the false creature Man.
The brief with weighty crimes was charged,
On which the pleader much enlarged;
That Cupid now has lost his art,
Or blunts the point of every dart;—
His altar now no longer smokes,
His mother's aid no youth invokes:
This tempts freethinkers to refine,
And bring in doubt their powers divine;
Now love is dwindled to intrigue,
And marriage grown a money league;
Which crimes aforesaid (with her leave)
Were (as he humbly did conceive)
Against our sovereign lady's peace,
Against the statute in that case,
Against her dignity and crown:
Then pray'd an answer, and sat down.
    The nymphs with scorn beheld their foes;
When the defendant's counsel rose,
And, what no lawyer ever lack'd,
With impudence own'd all the fact;
But, what the gentlest heart would vex,
Laid all the fault on t'other sex.
That modern love is no such thing
As what those ancient poets sing:
A fire celestial, chaste, refined,
Conceived and kindled in the mind;
Which, having found an equal flame,
Unites, and both become the same,
In different breasts together burn,
Together both to ashes turn.
But women now feel no such fire,
And only know the gross desire.

Their passions move in lower spheres,
Where'er caprice or folly steers,
A dog, a parrot, or an ape,
Or some worse brute in human shape,
Engross the fancies of the fair,
The few soft moments they can spare,
From visits to receive and pay,
From scandal, politics, and play;
From fans, and flounces, and brocades,
From equipage, and park parades,
From all the thousand female toys,
From every trifle that employs
The out or inside of their heads,
Between their toilets and their beds.

In a dull stream, which moving slow,
You hardly see the current flow;
If a small breeze obstruct the course,
It whirls about for want of force,
And in its narrow circle gathers
Nothing but chaff, and straws, and feathers.
The current of a female mind
Stops thus, and turns with every wind:
Thus whirling round together draws
Fools, fops, and rakes, for chaff and straws.
Hence we conclude, no women's hearts
Are won by virtue, wit, and parts:
Nor are the men of sense to blame,
For breasts incapable of flame;
The faults must on the nymphs be placed,
Grown so corrupted in their taste.

The pleader having spoke his best,
Had witness ready to attest,
Who fairly could on oath depose,
When questions on the fact arose,
That every article was true;
Nor further those deponents knew:
Therefore he humbly would insist,
The bill might be with costs dismiss'd.
The cause appear'd of so much weight,
That Venus, from her judgment seat,
Desired them not to talk so loud,
Else she must interpose a cloud:
For if the heavenly folks should know
These pleadings in the courts below,

That mortals here disdain to love,
She ne'er could show her face above;
For gods, their betters, are too wise
To value that which men despise.
And then, said she, my son and I
Must stroll in air, 'twixt land and sky;
Or else, shut out from heaven and earth,
Fly to the sea, my place of birth:
There live with daggled mermaids pent,
And keep on fish perpetual Lent.
But since the case appear'd so nice,
She thought it best to take advice.
The Muses, by the king's permission,
Though foes to love, attend the session,
And on the right hand took their places
In order; on the left, the Graces;
To whom she might her doubts propose
On all emergencies that rose.
The Muses oft were seen to frown;
The Graces half ashamed look'd down;
And 'twas observed, there were but few
Of either sex among the crew,
Whom she or her assessors knew.
The goddess soon began to see,
Things were not ripe for a decree;
And said, she must consult her books,
The lovers' Fletas, Bractons, Cokes.
First to a dapper clerk she beckon'd
To turn to Ovid, book the second;
She then referr'd them to a place
In Virgil, vide Dido's case:
As for Tibullus's reports,
They never pass'd for law in courts:
For Cowley's briefs, and pleas of Waller,
Still their authority was smaller.
　　There was on both sides much to say:
She'd hear the cause another day;
And so she did; and then a third;
She heard it—there she kept her word:
But, with rejoinders, or replies,
Long bills, and answers stuff'd with lies,
Demur, imparlance, and essoign,
The parties ne'er could issue join:
For sixteen years the cause was spun,

And then stood where it first begun.
Now, gentle Clio, sing, or say
What Venus meant by this delay?
The goddess much perplex'd in mind
To see her empire thus declined,
When first this grand debate arose,
Above her wisdom to compose,
Conceived a project in her head
To work her ends; which, if it sped,
Would show the merits of the cause
Far better than consulting laws.

In a glad hour Lucina's aid
Produced on earth a wondrous maid,
On whom the Queen of Love was bent,
To try a new experiment.
She threw her law-books on the shelf,
And thus debated with herself.

Since men allege they ne'er can find
Those beauties in a female mind,
Which raise a flame that will endure
For ever uncorrupt and pure;
If 'tis with reason they complain,
This infant shall restore my reign.
I'll search where every virtue dwells,
From courts inclusive down to cells:
What preachers talk, or sages write;
These will I gather and unite,
And represent them to mankind
Collected in that infant's mind.

This said, she plucks in Heaven's high bowers
A sprig of amaranthine flowers.
In nectar thrice infuses bays,
Three times refined in Titan's rays;
Then calls the Graces to her aid,
And sprinkles thrice the newborn maid:
From whence the tender skin assumes
A sweetness above all perfumes:
From whence a cleanliness remains,
Incapable of outward stains:
From whence that decency of mind,
So lovely in the female kind,
Where not one careless thought intrudes,
Less modest than the speech of prudes;
Where never blush was call'd in aid,

That spurious virtue in a maid,
A virtue but at second-hand;
They blush because they understand.
    The Graces next would act their part,
And show'd but little of their art;
Their work was half already done,
The child with native beauty shone;
The outward form no help required:
Each, breathing on her thrice, inspired
That gentle, soft, engaging air,
Which in old times adorn'd the fair:
And said, "Vanessa be the name
By which thou shalt be known to fame:
Vanessa, by the gods enroll'd:
Her name on earth shall not be told."
    But still the work was not complete;
When Venus thought on a deceit;
Drawn by her doves, away she flies,
And finds out Pallas in the skies.
Dear Pallas, I have been this morn
To see a lovely infant born:
A boy in yonder isle below,
So like my own without his bow,
By beauty could your heart be won,
You'd swear it is Apollo's son;
But it shall ne'er be said, a child
So hopeful, has by me been spoil'd:
I have enough besides to spare,
And give him wholly to your care.
    Wisdom's above suspecting wiles;
The Queen of Learning gravely smiles,
Down from Olympus comes with joy,
Mistakes Vanessa for a boy;
Then sows within her tender mind
Seeds long unknown to womankind:
For manly bosoms chiefly fit,
The seeds of knowledge, judgment, wit.
Her soul was suddenly endued
With justice, truth, and fortitude;
With honour, which no breath can stain,
Which malice must attack in vain;
With open heart and bounteous hand.
But Pallas here was at a stand;
She knew, in our degenerate days,

Bare virtue could not live on praise;
That meat must be with money bought:
She therefore, upon second thought,
Infused, yet as it were by stealth,
Some small regard for state and wealth:
Of which, as she grew up, there staid
A tincture in the prudent maid:
She managed her estate with care,
Yet liked three footmen to her chair,
But, lest he should neglect his studies
Like a young heir, the thrifty goddess
(For fear young master should be spoil'd)
Would use him like a younger child;
And, after long computing, found
'Twould come to just five thousand pound.

The Queen of Love was pleased, and proud,
To see Vanessa thus endow'd:
She doubted not but such a dame
Through every breast would dart a flame;
That every rich and lordly swain
With pride would drag about her chain;
That scholars would forsake their books,
To study bright Vanessa's looks:
As she advanced, that womankind
Would by her model form their mind,
And all their conduct would be tried
By her, as an unerring guide;
Offending daughters oft would hear
Vanessa's praise rung in their ear:
Miss Betty, when she does a fault,
Lets fall her knife, or spills the salt,
Will thus be by her mother chid,
" 'Tis what Vanessa never did!"
Thus by the nymphs and swains adored,
My power shall be again restored,
And happy lovers bless my reign—
So Venus hoped, but hoped in vain.

For when in time the Martial Maid
Found out the trick that Venus play'd,
She shakes her helm, she knits her brows,
And, fired with indignation, vows,
Tomorrow, ere the setting sun,
She'll all undo that she had done.

But in the poets we may find

A wholesome law, time out of mind,
Had been confirm'd by Fate's decree,
That gods, of whatsoe'er degree,
Resume not what themselves have given,
Or any brother god in Heaven:
Which keeps the peace among the gods,
Or they must always be at odds:
And Pallas, if she broke the laws,
Must yield her foe the stronger cause;
A shame to one so much adored
For wisdom at Jove's council-board.
Besides, she fear'd the Queen of Love
Would meet with better friends above.
And though she must with grief reflect,
To see a mortal virgin deck'd
With graces hitherto unknown
To female breasts, except her own:
Yet she would act as best became
A goddess of unspotted fame.
She knew, by augury divine,
Venus would fail in her design:
She studied well the point, and found
Her foe's conclusions were not sound,
From premises erroneous brought,
And therefore the deduction's naught,
And must have contrary effects,
To what her treacherous foe expects.
    In proper season Pallas meets
The Queen of Love, whom thus she greets,
(For gods, we are by Homer told,
Can in celestial language scold:)—
Perfidious goddess! but in vain
You form'd this project in your brain;
A project for your talents fit,
With much deceit and little wit.
Thou hast, as thou shalt quickly see,
Deceived thyself, instead of me;
For how can heavenly wisdom prove
An instrument to earthly love?
Know'st thou not yet, that men commence
Thy votaries for want of sense?
Nor shall Vanessa be the theme
To manage thy abortive scheme;
She'll prove the greatest of thy foes;

And yet I scorn to interpose,
But, using neither skill nor force,
Leave all things to their natural course.

The goddess thus pronounced her doom:
When, lo! Vanessa in her bloom
Advanced, like Atalanta's star,
But rarely seen, and seen from far:
In a new world with caution stept,
Watch'd all the company she kept,
Well knowing, from the books she read,
What dangerous paths young virgins tread:
Would seldom at the Park appear,
Nor saw the play-house twice a year;
Yet, not incurious, was inclined
To know the converse of mankind.

First issued from perfumers' shops,
A crowd of fashionable fops:
They asked her how she liked the play;
Then told the tattle of the day;
A duel fought last night at two,
About a lady—you know who;
Mention'd a new Italian, come
Either from Muscovy or Rome;
Gave hints of who and who's together;
Then fell to talking of the weather;
Last night was so extremely fine,
The ladies walk'd till after nine:
Then, in soft voice and speech absurd,
With nonsense every second word,
With fustian from exploded plays,
They celebrate her beauty's praise;
Run o'er their cant of stupid lies,
And tell the murders of her eyes.

With silent scorn Vanessa sat,
Scarce listening to their idle chat;
Farther than sometimes by a frown,
When they grew pert, to pull them down.
At last she spitefully was bent
To try their wisdom's full extent;
And said, she valued nothing less
Than titles, figure, shape, and dress;
That merit should be chiefly placed
In judgment, knowledge, wit, and taste;
And these, she offer'd to dispute,

Alone distinguished man from brute:
That present times have no pretence
To virtue, in the noble sense
By Greeks and Romans understood,
To perish for our country's good.
She named the ancient heroes round,
Explain'd for what they were renown'd;
Then spoke with censure or applause
Of foreign customs, rites, and laws;
Through nature and through art she ranged,
And gracefully her subject changed;
In vain! her hearers had no share
In all she spoke, except to stare.
Their judgment was, upon the whole,
—That lady is the dullest soul!—
Then tapt their forehead in a jeer,
As who should say—She wants it here!
She may be handsome, young, and rich,
But none will burn her for a witch!

    A party next of glittering dames,
From round the purlieus of St. James,
Came early, out of pure good will,
To see the girl in dishabille.
Their clamour, 'lighting from their chairs,
Grew louder all the way upstairs;
At entrance loudest, where they found
The room with volumes litter'd round.
Vanessa held Montaigne, and read,
While Mrs. Susan comb'd her head.
They call'd for tea and chocolate,
And fell into their usual chat,
Discoursing with important face,
On ribbons, fans, and gloves, and lace;
Show'd patterns just from India brought,
And gravely ask'd her what she thought,
Whether the red or green were best,
And what they cost? Vanessa guess'd
As came into her fancy first:
Named half the rates, and liked the worst.
To scandal next—What awkward thing
Was that last Sunday in the ring?
I'm sorry Mopsa breaks so fast:
I said her face would never last.
Corinna, with that youthful air,

Is thirty, and a bit to spare:
Her fondness for a certain earl
Began when I was but a girl!
Phillis, who but a month ago
Was married to the Tonbridge beau,
I saw coquetting t'other night
In public with that odious knight!

      They rallied next Vanessa's dress;
That gown was made for old Queen Bess.
Dear madam, let me see your head:
Don't you intend to put on red?
A petticoat without a hoop!
Sure, you are not ashamed to stoop!
With handsome garters at your knees,
No matter what a fellow sees.

      Fill'd with disdain, with rage inflamed,
Both of herself and sex ashamed,
The nymph stood silent out of spite,
Nor would vouchsafe to set them right.
Away the fair detractors went,
And gave by turns their censures vent.
She's not so handsome in my eyes:
For wit, I wonder where it lies!
She's fair and clean, and that's the most:
But why proclaim her for a toast?
A baby face; no life, no airs,
But what she learn'd at country fairs;
Scarce knows what difference is between
Rich Flanders lace and Colberteen.
I'll undertake, my little Nancy
In flounces has a better fancy;
With all her wit, I would not ask
Her judgment how to buy a mask.
We begg'd her but to patch her face,
She never hit one proper place;
Which every girl at five years old
Can do as soon as she is told.
I own, that out-of-fashion stuff
Becomes the creature well enough.
The girl might pass, if we could get her
To know the world a little better.
(To know the world! a modern phrase
For visits, ombre, balls, and plays.)

      Thus, to the world's perpetual shame,

The Queen of Beauty lost her aim;
Too late with grief she understood
Pallas had done more harm than good;
For great examples are but vain,
Where ignorance begets disdain.
Both sexes, arm'd with guilt and spite,
Against Vanessa's power unite:
To copy her few nymphs aspired;
Her virtues fewer swains admired.
So stars, beyond a certain height,
Give mortals neither heat nor light.
Yet some of either sex, endow'd
With gifts superior to the crowd,
With virtue, knowledge, taste, and wit,
She condescended to admit:
With pleasing arts she could reduce
Men's talents to their proper use;
And with address each genius held
To that wherein it most excell'd;
Thus, making others' wisdom known,
Could please them and improve her own.
A modest youth said something new;
She placed it in the strongest view.
All humble worth she strove to raise,
Would not be praised, yet loved to praise.
The learned met with free approach,
Although they came not in a coach:
Some clergy too she would allow,
Nor quarrell'd at their awkward bow;
But this was for Cadenus' sake,
A gownman of a different make;
Whom Pallas once, Vanessa's tutor,
Had fix'd on for her coadjutor.
    But Cupid, full of mischief, longs
To vindicate his mother's wrongs.
On Pallas all attempts are vain:
One way he knows to give her pain;
Vows on Vanessa's heart to take
Due vengeance, for her patron's sake;
Those early seeds by Venus sown,
In spite of Pallas now were grown;
And Cupid hoped they would improve
By time, and ripen into love.
The boy made use of all his craft,

In vain discharging many a shaft,
Pointed at colonels, lords, and beaux:
Cadenus warded off the blows;
For, placing still some book betwixt,
The darts were in the cover fix'd,
Or often blunted and recoil'd,
On Plutarch's Morals struck, were spoil'd.

    The Queen of Wisdom could foresee,
But not prevent, the Fates' decree:
And human caution tries in vain
To break that adamantine chain.
Vanessa, though by Pallas taught,
By Love invulnerable thought,
Searching in books for wisdom's aid,
Was in the very search betray'd.

    Cupid, though all his darts were lost,
Yet still resolved to spare no cost:
He could not answer to his fame
The triumphs of that stubborn dame,
A nymph so hard to be subdued,
Who neither was coquette nor prude.
I find, said he, she wants a doctor,
Both to adore her, and instruct her:
I'll give her what she most admires
Among those venerable sires.
Cadenus is a subject fit
Grown old in politics and wit,
Caress'd by ministers of state,
Of half mankind the dread and hate.
Whate'er vexations love attend,
She needs no rivals apprehend;
Her sex, with universal voice,
Must laugh at her capricious choice.

    Cadenus many things had writ:
Vanessa much esteem'd his wit,
And call'd for his poetic works:
Meantime the boy in secret lurks;
And, while the book was in her hand,
The urchin from his private stand
Took aim, and shot with all his strength
A dart of such prodigious length,
It pierced the feeble volume through,
And deep transfix'd her bosom too.
Some lines, more moving than the rest,

Stuck to the point that pierced her breast,
And, borne directly to the heart,
With pains unknown increased her smart.
    Vanessa, not in years a score,
Dreams of a gown of forty-four;
Imaginary charms can find
In eyes with reading almost blind:
Cadenus now no more appears
Declined in health, advanced in years.
She fancies music in his tongue:
Nor farther looks, but thinks him young.
What mariner is not afraid
To venture in a ship decay'd?
What planter will attempt to yoke
A sapling with a falling oak?
As years increase, she brighter shines;
Cadenus with each day declines:
And he must fall a prey to time
While she continues in her prime.
Cadenus, common forms apart,
In every scene had kept his heart;
Had sigh'd and languish'd, vow'd and writ,
For pastime, or to show his wit,
But books, and time, and state affairs,
Had spoil'd his fashionable airs:
He now could praise, esteem, approve,
But understood not what was love.
His conduct might have made him styled
A father, and the nymph his child.
The innocent delight he took
To see the virgin mind her book,
Was but the master's secret joy
In school to hear the finest boy.
Her knowledge with her fancy grew;
She hourly press'd for something new;
Ideas came into her mind
So fast, his lessons lagg'd behind;
She reason'd, without plodding long,
Nor ever gave her judgment wrong.
But now a sudden change was wrought;
She minds no longer what he taught;
Cadenus was amazed to find
Such marks of a distracted mind:
For, though she seem'd to listen more

To all he spoke, than e'er before,
He found her thoughts would absent range,
Yet guess'd not whence could spring the change.
And first he modestly conjectures
His pupil might be tired with lectures;
Which help'd to mortify his pride,
Yet gave him not the heart to chide:
But, in a mild, dejected strain,
At last he ventured to complain:
Said, she should be no longer teased,
Might have her freedom when she pleased;
Was now convinced he acted wrong
To hide her from the world so long,
And in dull studies to engage
One of her tender sex and age;
That every nymph with envy own'd
How she might shine in the grand monde:
And every shepherd is undone
To see her cloister'd like a nun.
This was a visionary scheme:
He waked, and found it but a dream;
A project far above his skill:
For nature must be nature still.
If he were bolder than became
A scholar to a courtly dame,
She might excuse a man of letters;
Thus tutors often treat their betters:
And, since his talk offensive grew,
He came to take his last adieu.

      Vanessa, fill'd with just disdain,
Would still her dignity maintain,
Instructed from her early years
To scorn the art of female tears.

      Had he employ'd his time so long
To teach her what was right and wrong;
Yet could such notions entertain
That all his lectures were in vain?
She own'd the wandering of her thoughts;
But he must answer for her faults.
She well remember'd to her cost,
That all his lessons were not lost.
Two maxims she could still produce,
And sad experience taught their use;
That virtue, pleased by being shown,

Knows nothing which it dares not own;
Can make us without fear disclose
Our inmost secrets to our foes;
That common forms were not design'd
Directors to a noble mind.
Now, said the nymph, to let you see
My actions with your rules agree;
That I can vulgar forms despise,
And have no secrets to disguise;
I knew, by what you said and writ,
How dangerous things were men of wit;
You caution'd me against their charms,
But never gave me equal arms;
Your lessons found the weakest part,
Aim'd at the head, but reach'd the heart.

    Cadenus felt within him rise
Shame, disappointment, guilt, surprise.
He knew not how to reconcile
Such language with her usual style;
And yet her words were so exprest,
He could not hope she spoke in jest.
His thoughts had wholly been confined
To form and cultivate her mind.
He hardly knew, till he was told,
Whether the nymph were young or old;
Had met her in a public place,
Without distinguishing her face;
Much less could his declining age
Vanessa's earliest thoughts engage;
And, if her youth indifference met,
His person must contempt beget;
Or grant her passion be sincere,
How shall his innocence be clear?
Appearances were all so strong,
The world must think him in the wrong;
Would say, he made a treacherous use
Of wit, to flatter and seduce;
The town would swear he had betray'd
By magic spells the harmless maid:
And every beau would have his jokes,
That scholars were like other folks;
And, when Platonic flights were over,
The tutor turn'd a mortal lover!
So tender of the young and fair!

It show'd a true paternal care—
Five thousand guineas in her purse!
The doctor might have fancied worse.—
    Hardly at length he silence broke,
And falter'd every word he spoke;
Interpreting her complaisance,
Just as a man sans consequence.
She rallied well, he always knew;
Her manner now was something new;
And what she spoke was in an air
As serious as a tragic player.
But those who aim at ridicule
Should fix upon some certain rule,
Which fairly hints they are in jest,
Else he must enter his protest:
For let a man be ne'er so wise,
He may be caught with sober lies;
A science which he never taught,
And, to be free, was dearly bought;
For, to take it in its proper light,
'Tis just what coxcombs call a bite.
    But, not to dwell on things minute,
Vanessa finish'd the dispute;
Brought weighty arguments to prove
That reason was her guide in love.
She thought he had himself described,
His doctrines when she first imbibed;
What he had planted, now was grown;
His virtues she might call her own;
As he approves, as he dislikes,
Love or contempt her fancy strikes.
Self-love, in nature rooted fast,
Attends us first and leaves us last;
Why she likes him, admire not at her;
She loves herself, and that's the matter.
How was her tutor wont to praise
The geniuses of ancient days!
(Those authors he so oft had named,
For learning, wit, and wisdom, famed;)
Was struck with love, esteem, and awe,
For persons whom he never saw.
Suppose Cadenus flourish'd then,
He must adore such godlike men.
If one short volume could comprise

All that was witty, learn'd, and wise,
How would it be esteemed and read,
Although the writer long were dead!
If such an author were alive,
How all would for his friendship strive,
And come in crowds to see his face!
And this she takes to be her case.
Cadenus answers every end,
The book, the author, and the friend;
The utmost her desires will reach,
Is but to learn what he can teach:
His converse is a system fit
Alone to fill up all her wit;
While every passion of her mind
In him is centered and confined.

Love can with speech inspire a mute,
And taught Vanessa to dispute.
This topic, never touch'd before,
Display'd her eloquence the more:
Her knowledge, with such pains acquir'd,
By this new passion grew inspired;
Through this she made all objects pass,
Which gave a tincture o'er the mass;
As rivers, though they bend and twine,
Still to the sea their course incline:
Or, as philosophers who find
Some favourite system to their mind,
In every point to make it fit,
Will force all nature to submit.

Cadenus, who could ne'er suspect
His lessons would have such effect,
Or be so artfully applied,
Insensibly came on her side.
It was an unforeseen event;
Things took a turn he never meant.
Whoe'er excels in what we prize
Appears a hero in our eyes;
Each girl, when pleased with what is taught,
Will have the teacher in her thought.
When miss delights in her spinet,
A fiddler may a fortune get;
A blockhead, with melodious voice,
In boarding-schools may have his choice:
And oft the dancing-master's art

Climbs from the toe to touch the heart.
In learning let a nymph delight,
The pedant gets a mistress by't.
Cadenus, to his grief and shame,
Could scarce oppose Vanessa's flame;
And, though her arguments were strong,
At least could hardly wish them wrong.
Howe'er it came, he could not tell,
But sure she never talk'd so well.
His pride began to interpose;
Preferr'd before a crowd of beaux!
So bright a nymph to come unsought!
Such wonder by his merit wrought!
'Tis merit must with her prevail!
He never knew her judgment fail!
She noted all she ever read!
And had a most discerning head!
 'Tis an old maxim in the schools,
That flattery's the food of fools;
Yet now and then your men of wit
Will condescend to take a bit.
 So when Cadenus could not hide,
He chose to justify his pride;
Construing the passion she had shown,
Much to her praise, more to his own.
Nature in him had merit placed,
In her a most judicious taste.
Love, hitherto a transient guest,
Ne'er held possession of his breast;
So long attending at the gate,
Disdain'd to enter in so late.
Love why do we one passion call,
When 'tis a compound of them all?
Where hot and cold, where sharp and sweet,
In all their equipages meet;
Where pleasures mix'd with pains appear,
Sorrow with joy, and hope with fear;
Wherein his dignity and age
Forbid Cadenus to engage.
But friendship, in its greatest height,
A constant, rational delight,
On virtue's basis fix'd to last,
When love allurements long are past,
Which gently warms, but cannot burn,

He gladly offers in return;
His want of passion will redeem
With gratitude, respect, esteem:
With what devotion we bestow,
When goddesses appear below.
    While thus Cadenus entertains
Vanessa in exalted strains,
The nymph in sober words entreats
A truce with all sublime conceits;
For why such raptures, flights, and fancies,
To her who durst not read romances?
In lofty style to make replies,
Which he had taught her to despise?
But when her tutor will affect
Devotion, duty, and respect,
He fairly abdicates the throne:
The government is now her own;
He has a forfeiture incurr'd;
She vows to take him at his word,
And hopes he will not think it strange,
If both should now their stations change;
The nymph will have her turn to be
The tutor; and the pupil, he;
Though she already can discern
Her scholar is not apt to learn;
Or wants capacity to reach
The science she designs to teach;
Wherein his genius was below
The skill of every common beau,
Who, though he cannot spell, is wise
Enough to read a lady's eyes,
And will each accidental glance
Interpret for a kind advance.
    But what success Vanessa met
Is to the world a secret yet.
Whether the nymph, to please her swain,
Talks in a high romantic strain;
Or whether he at last descends
To act with less seraphic ends;
Or to compound the business, whether
They temper love and books together;
Must never to mankind be told,
Nor shall the conscious Muse unfold.
    Meantime the mournful Queen of Love

Led but a weary life above.
She ventures now to leave the skies,
Grown by Vanessa's conduct wise:
For though by one perverse event
Pallas had cross'd her first intent;
Though her design was not obtain'd:
Yet had she much experience gain'd,
And, by the project vainly tried,
Could better now the cause decide.
She gave due notice, that both parties,
Coram Regina, prox' die Martis,
Should at their peril, without fail,
Come and appear, and save their bail.
All met; and, silence thrice proclaim'd,
One lawyer to each side was named.
The judge discover'd in her face
Resentments for her late disgrace;
And full of anger, shame, and grief,
Directed them to mind their brief;
Nor spend their time to show their reading:
She'd have a summary proceeding.
She gather'd under every head
The sum of what each lawyer said,
Gave her own reasons last, and then
Decreed the cause against the men.

But in a weighty case like this,
To show she did not judge amiss,
Which evil tongues might else report,
She made a speech in open court;
Wherein she grievously complains,
"How she was cheated by the swains;
On whose petition (humbly showing,
That women were not worth the wooing,
And that, unless the sex would mend,
The race of lovers soon must end)—
She was at Lord knows what expense
To form a nymph of wit and sense,
A model for her sex design'd,
Who never could one lover find.
She saw her favour was misplaced;
The fellows had a wretched taste;
She needs must tell them to their face,
They were a stupid, senseless race;
And, were she to begin again,

She'd study to reform the men;
Or add some grains of folly more
To women, than they had before,
To put them on an equal foot;
And this, or nothing else, would do't.
This might their mutual fancy strike;
Since every being loves its like.

"But now, repenting what was done,
She left all business to her son;
She put the world in his possession,
And let him use it at discretion."

The crier was order'd to dismiss
The court, so made his last "O yes!"
The goddess would no longer wait;
But, rising from her chair of state,
Left all below at six and seven,
Harness'd her doves, and flew to Heaven.

axial
disorder

Swift and Mankind

A Description of the Morning

Now hardly here and there a hackney-coach _(taxi)_
Appearing, show'd the ruddy morn's approach.
Now Betty from her master's bed had flown,
And softly stole to discompose her own _(slip her own bed)_
The slip-shod 'prentice from his master's door
Had pared the dirt, and sprinkled round the floor.
Now Moll had whirl'd her mop with dext'rous airs,
Prepared to scrub the entry and the stairs.
The youth with broomy stumps began to trace
The kennel-edge, where wheels had worn the place.
The small-coal man was heard with cadence deep,
Till drown'd in shriller notes of chimney-sweep:
Duns at his lordship's gate began to meet;
And brickdust Moll had scream'd through half the street.
The turnkey now his flock returning sees,
Duly let out a-nights to steal for fees:
The watchful bailiffs take their silent stands,
And schoolboys lag with satchels in their hands.

An Elegy

On the Death of Demar, the Usurer

Know all men by these presents, Death, the tamer,
By mortgage has secured the corpse of Demar;
Nor can four hundred thousand sterling pound
Redeem him from his prison under ground.
His heirs might well, of all his wealth possess'd,
Bestow, to bury him, one iron chest.
Plutus, the god of wealth, will joy to know
His faithful steward in the shades below.
He walk'd the streets, and wore a threadbare cloak;
He dined and supped at charge of other folk:
And by his looks, had he held out his palms,
He might be thought an object fit for alms.
So, to the poor if he refused his pelf,
He used them full as kindly as himself.

Where'er he went, he never saw his betters;
Lords, knights, and squires, were all his humble debtors;
And under hand and seal, the Irish nation
Were forced to own to him their obligation.

He that could once have half a kingdom bought,
In half a minute is not worth a groat.
His coffers from the coffin could not save,
Nor all his interest keep him from the grave.
A golden monument would not be right,
Because we wish the earth upon him light.

Oh London Tavern! Thou hast lost a friend,
Though in thy walls he ne'er did farthing spend;
He touch'd the pence when others touch'd the pot;
The hand that signed the mortgage paid the shot.

Old as he was, no vulgar known disease
On him could ever boast a power to seize;
But as he weighed his gold, grim Death in spite
Cast in his dart, which made three moidores light;
And, as he saw his darling money fail,
Blew his last breath to sink the lighter scale.
He who so long was current, 'twould be strange
If he should now be cried down since his change.

The sexton shall green sods on thee bestow;
Alas, the sexton is thy banker now!
A dismal banker must that banker be,
Who gives no bills but of mortality!

The Description of a Salamander

As mastiff dogs, in modern phrase, are
Call'd Pompey, Scipio, and Caesar;
As pies and daws are often styled
With Christian nicknames, like a child;
As we say Monsieur to an ape,
Without offence to human shape;
So men have got, from bird and brute,
Names that would best their nature suit.
The Lion, Eagle, Fox, and Boar,
Were heroes' titles heretofore,
Bestow'd as hieroglyphics fit
To show their valour, strength, or wit:
For what is understood by fame,
Besides the getting of a name?
But, e'er since men invented guns,
A different way their fancy runs:
To paint a hero, we inquire
For something that will conquer fire.
Would you describe Turenne or Trump?
Think of a bucket or a pump.
Are these too low?—Then find out grander,
Call my Lord Cutts a Salamander.
'Tis well;—but since we live among
Detractors with an evil tongue,
Who may object against the term,
Pliny shall prove what we affirm:
Pliny shall prove, and we'll apply,
And I'll be judg'd by standers by

First, then, our author has defined
This reptile of the serpent kind,
With gaudy coat, and shining train;
But loathsome spots his body stain:
Out from some hole obscure he flies,
When rains descend, and tempests rise,
Till the sun clears the air; and then
Crawls back neglected to his den.

So, when the war has raised a storm,
I've seen a snake in human form,
All stain'd with infamy and vice,
Leap from the dunghill in a trice,
Burnish and make a gaudy show,
Become a general, peer, and beau,

Till peace has made the sky serene,
Then shrink into its hole again.
"All this we grant—why then, look yonder,
Sure that must be a Salamander!"
    Further, we are by Pliny told,
This serpent is extremely cold;
So cold, that put it in the fire,
'Twill make the very flames expire:
Besides, it spews a filthy froth
(Whether through rage or love, or both)
Of matter purulent and white,
Which, happening on the skin to light,
And there corrupting to a wound,
Spreads leprosy and baldness round.
    So I have seen a batter'd beau,
By age and claps grown cold as snow,
Whose breath or touch, where'er he came,
Blew out love's torch, or chill'd the flame:
And should some nymph, who ne'er was cruel,
Like Carleton cheap, or famed Du-Ruel,
Receive the filth which he ejects,
She soon would find the same effects,
Her tainted carcase to pursue,
As from the Salamander's spew;
A dismal shedding of her locks,
And, if no leprosy, a pox.
"Then I'll appeal to each bystander,
If this be not a Salamander?"

A Beautiful Young Nymph Going to Bed

Corinna, pride of Drury-Lane,
For whom no shepherd sighs in vain;
Never did Covent-Garden boast
So bright a batter'd strolling toast!
No drunken rake to pick her up,
No cellar where on tick to sup;
Returning at the midnight hour,
Four stories climbing to her bower;
Then, seated on a three-legg'd chair,
Takes off her artificial hair;
Now picking out a crystal eye,
She wipes it clean, and lays it by.
Her eyebrows from a mouse's hide
Stuck on with art on either side,
Pulls off with care, and first displays 'em,
Then in a play-book smoothly lays 'em.
Now dext'rously her plumpers draws,
That serve to fill her hollow jaws,
Untwists a wire, and from her gums
A set of teeth completely comes;
Pulls out the rags contrived to prop
Her flabby dugs, and down they drop.
Proceeding on, the lovely goddess
Unlaces next her steel-ribb'd bodice,
Which, by the operator's skill,
Press down the lumps, the hollows fill.
Up goes her hand, and off she slips
The bolsters that supply her hips:
With gentlest touch she next explores
Her chancres, issues, running sores;
Effects of many a sad disaster,
And then to each applies a plaster:
But must, before she goes to bed,
Rub off the daubs of white and red,
And smooth the furrows in her front
With greasy paper stuck upon't.
She takes a bolus ere she sleeps;
And then between two blankets creeps.
With pains of love tormented lies;
Or, if she chance to close her eyes,
Of Bridewell and the Compter dreams,
And feels the lash, and faintly screams;

Or by a faithless bully drawn,
At some hedge-tavern lies in pawn;
Or to Jamaica seems transported
Alone, and by no planter courted;
Or, near Fleet-ditch's oozy brinks,
Surrounded with a hundred stinks,
Belated, seems on watch to lie,
And snap some cully passing by;
Or, struck with fear, her fancy runs
On watchmen, constables, and duns,
From whom she meets with frequent rubs;
But never from religious clubs;
Whose favour she is sure to find,
Because she pays them all in kind.
  Corinna wakes. A dreadful sight!
Behold the ruins of the night!
A wicked rat her plaster stole,
Half eat, and dragg'd it to his hole.
The crystal eye, alas! was missed;
And puss had on her plumpers p-ss'd.
A pigeon picked her issue-pease:
And Shock her tresses fill'd with fleas.
  The nymph, though in this mangled plight,
Must every morn her limbs unite.
But how shall I describe her arts
To re-collect the scatter'd parts?
Or show the anguish, toil, and pain,
Of gathering up herself again?
The bashful Muse will never bear
In such a scene to interfere.
Corinna, in the morning dizen'd,
Who sees, will spew; who smells, be poison'd.

Phyllis

Or, The Progress of Love

Desponding Phyllis was endued
With every talent of a prude:
She trembled when a man drew near;
Salute her, and she turn'd her ear:
If o'er against her you were placed,
She durst not look above your waist:
She'd rather take you to her bed,
Than let you see her dress her head;
In church you hear her, through the crowd,
Repeat the absolution loud:
In church, secure behind her fan,
She durst behold that monster man:
There practised how to place her head,
And bite her lips to make them red;
Or, on the mat devoutly kneeling,
Would lift her eyes up to the ceiling.
And heave her bosom unaware,
For neighbouring beaux to see it bare.

    At length a lucky lover came,
And found admittance to the dame.
Suppose all parties now agreed,
The writings drawn, the lawyer fee'd,
The vicar and the ring bespoke:
Guess, how could such a match be broke?
See then what mortals place their bliss in!
Next morn betimes the bride was missing:
The mother screamed, the father chid;
Where can this idle wench be hid?
No news of Phyl! the bridegroom came,
And thought his bride had skulk'd for shame;
Because her father used to say,
The girl had such a bashful way!

    Now John the butler must be sent
To learn the road that Phyllis went:
The groom was wish'd to saddle Crop;
For John must neither light nor stop,
But find her whereso'er she fled,
And bring her back alive or dead.
    See here again the devil to do!

For truly John was missing too:
The horse and pillion both were gone!
Phyllis, it seems, was fled with John.
    Old Madam, who went up to find
What papers Phyl had left behind,
A letter on the toilet sees,
"To my much-honoured father—these—"
('Tis always done, romances tell us,
When daughters run away with fellows,)
Fill'd with the choicest common-places,
By others used in the like cases.
"That long ago a fortune-teller
Exactly said what now befell her;
And in a glass had made her see
A serving-man of low degree.
It was her fate, must be forgiven;
For marriages were made in Heaven:
His pardon begg'd: but, to be plain,
She'd do't if 'twere to do again:
For John was come of honest kin.
Love never thinks of rich and poor;
She'd beg with John from door to door.
Forgive her, if it be a crime;
She'll never do't another time.
She ne'er before in all her life
Once disobey'd him, maid nor wife."
One argument she summ'd up all in,
"The thing was done and past recalling;
And therefore hoped she should recover
His favour when his passion's over.
She valued not what others thought her,
And was—his most obedient daughter."
Fair maidens all, attend the Muse,
Who now the wandering pair pursues:
Away they rode in homely sort,
Their journey long, their money short;
The loving couple well bemired;
The horse and both the riders tired:
Their victuals bad, their lodgings worse;
Phyl cried! and John began to curse:
Phyl wish'd that she had strain'd a limb,
When first she ventured out with him;
John wish'd that he had broke a leg,

When first for her he quitted Peg.
　　But what adventures more befell them,
The Muse has now no time to tell them;
How Johnny wheedled, threaten'd, fawn'd,
Till Phyllis all her trinkets pawn'd:
How oft she broke her marriage vows,
In kindness to maintain her spouse,
Till swains unwholesome spoil'd the trade;
For now the surgeons must be paid,
To whom those perquisites are gone,
In Christian justice due to John.
　　When food and raiment now grew scarce,
Fate put a period to the farce,
And with exact poetic justice;
For John was landlord, Phyllis hostess;
They keep, at Stains, the Old Blue Boar,
Are cat and dog, and rogue and whore.

The farmer's goose, who in the stubble
Has fed without restraint or trouble,
Grown fat with corn and sitting still,
Can scarce get o'er the barn-door sill;
And hardly waddles forth to cool
Her belly in the neighbouring pool!
Nor loudly cackles at the door;
For cackling shows the goose is poor.
　　But, when she must be turn'd to graze,
And round the barren common strays,
Hard exercise, and harder fare,
Soon make my dame grow lank and spare;
Her body light, she tries her wings,
And scorns the ground, and upward springs
While all the parish, as she flies,
Hear sounds harmonious from the skies.
　　Such is the poet fresh in pay,
The third night's profits of his play;
His morning draughts till noon can swill,
Among his brethren of the quill:
With good roast beef his belly full.
Grown lazy, foggy, fat, and dull,
Deep sunk in plenty and delight,
What poet e'er could take his flight?
Or, stuff'd with phlegm up to the throat,
What poet e'er could sing a note?
Nor Pegasus could bear the load
Along the high celestial road;
The steed, oppress'd, would break his girth,
To raise the lumber from the earth.
　　But view him in another scene,
When all his drink is Hippocrene,
His money spent, his patrons fail,
His credit out for cheese and ale;
His two-years' coat so smooth and bare,
Through every thread it lets in air;
With hungry meals his body pined,
His guts and belly full of wind;
And, like a jockey for a race,
His flesh brought down to flying case:
Now his exalted spirit loathes

Encumbrances of food and clothes;
And up he rises like a vapour,
Supported high on wings of paper.
He singing flies, and flying sings,
While from below all Grub-Street rings.

Helter Skelter

Or, the Hue and Cry after the Attorneys upon their Riding
the Circuit

> Now the active young attorneys
> Briskly travel on their journeys,
> Looking big as any giants,
> On the horses of their clients;
> Like so many little Marses
> With their tilters at their arses,
> Brazen-hilted, lately burnish'd,
> And with harness-buckles furnished,
> And with whips and spurs so neat,
> And with jockey-coats complete,
> And with boots so very greasy,
> And with saddles eke so easy,
> And with bridles fine and gay,
> Bridles borrow'd for a day,
> Bridles destined far to roam,
> Ah! never, never to come home.
> And with hats so very big, sir,
> And with powder'd caps and wigs, sir,
> And with ruffles to be shown,
> Cambric ruffles not their own;
> And with Holland shirts so white,
> Shirts becoming to the sight,
> Shirts bewrought with different letters,
> As belonging to their betters.
> With their pretty tinsel'd boxes,
> Gotten from their dainty doxies,
> And with rings so very trim,
> Lately taken out of lim—
> And with very little pence,
> And as very little sense;
> With some law, but little justice,
> Having stolen from my hostess,
> From the barber and the cutler,
> Like the soldier from the sutler;
> From the vintner and the tailor,
> Like the felon from the jailor;
> Into this and t'other county,
> Living on the public bounty;

Thorough town and thorough village,
All to plunder, all to pillage:
Thorough mountains, thorough valleys,
Thorough stinking lanes and alleys,
Some to—kiss with farmers' spouses,
And make merry in their houses;
Some to tumble country wenches
On their rushy beds and benches;
And if they begin a fray,
Draw their swords, and—run away;
All to murder equity,
And to take a double fee;
Till the people are all quiet,
And forget to broil and riot,
Low in pocket, cow'd in courage,
Safely glad to sup their porridge,
And vacation's over—then,
Hey, for London town again.

The Progress of Marriage

Aetatis suae fifty-two,
A rich divine began to woo
A handsome, young, imperious girl,
Nearly related to an earl.
Her parents and her friends consent;
The couple to the temple went:
They first invite the Cyprian queen;
'Twas answered, "She would not be seen;"
The Graces next, and all the Muses,
Were bid in form, but sent excuses.
Juno attended at the porch,
With farthing candle for a torch;
While mistress Iris held her train,
The faded bow distilling rain.
Then Hebe came, and took her place,
But show'd no more than half her face.

    Whate'er those dire forebodings meant,
In mirth the wedding-day was spent;
The wedding-day, you take me right,
I promise nothing for the night.
The bridegroom, drest to make a figure,
Assumes an artificial vigour;
A flourish'd nightcap on, to grace
His ruddy, wrinkled, smiling face;
Like the faint red upon a pippin,
Half wither'd by a winter's keeping.

    And thus set out this happy pair,
The swain is rich, the nymph is fair;
But, what I gladly would forget,
The swain is old, the nymph coquette.
Both from the goal together start;
Scarce run a step before they part;
No common ligament that binds
The various textures of their minds;
Their thoughts and actions, hopes and fears,
Less corresponding than their years.
Her spouse desires his coffee soon,
She rises to her tea at noon.
While he goes out to cheapen books,
She at the glass consults her looks;
While Betty's buzzing in her ear,
Lord, what a dress these parsons wear!

So odd a choice how could she make!
Wish'd him a colonel for her sake.
Then, on her finger ends she counts,
Exact, to what his age amounts.
The Dean, she heard her uncle say,
Is sixty, if he be a day;
His ruddy cheeks are no disguise;
You see the crow's feet round his eyes.

 At one she rambles to the shops,
To cheapen tea, and talk with fops;
Or calls a council of her maids,
And tradesmen to compare brocades.
Her weighty morning business o'er,
Sits down to dinner just at four;
Minds nothing that is done or said,
Her evening work so fills her head.
The Dean who used to dine at one,
Is mawkish, and his stomach's gone;
In threadbare gown, would scarce a louse hold,
Looks like the chaplain of his household;
Beholds her, from the chaplain's place,
In French brocades, and Flanders lace;
He wonders what employs her brain,
But never asks, or asks in vain;
His mind is full of other cares,
And, in the sneaking parson's airs,
Computes, that half a parish dues
Will hardly find his wife in shoes.

 Canst thou imagine, dull divine,
'Twill gain her love, to make her fine?
Hath she no other wants beside?
You raise desire as well as pride,
Enticing coxcombs to adore,
And teach her to despise thee more.

 If in her coach she'll condescend
To place him at the hinder end,
Her hoop is hoist above his nose,
His odious gown would soil her clothes,
And drops him at the church, to pray,
While she drives on to see the play.
He, like an orderly divine,
Comes home a quarter after nine,
And meets her hasting to the ball;
Her chairmen push him from the wall.

He enters in, and walks up stairs,
And calls the family to prayers;
Then goes alone to take his rest
In bed, where he can spare her best.
At five the footmen make a din,
Her ladyship is just come in;
The masquerade began at two,
She stole away with much ado;
And shall be chid this afternoon,
For leaving company so soon:
She'll say, and she may truly say't,
She can't abide to stay out late.

But now, though scarce a twelvemonth married,
Poor Lady Jane has thrice miscarried:
The cause, alas! is quickly guest;
The town has whisper'd round the jest,
Think on some remedy in time,
You find his reverence past his prime,
Already dwindled to a lath:
No other way but try the bath.

For Venus, rising from the ocean,
Infused a strong prolific potion,
That mix'd with Acheloüs spring,
The horned flood, as poets sing,
Who, with an English beauty smitten,
Ran under ground from Greece to Britain;
The genial virtue with him brought,
And gave the nymph a plenteous draught;
Then fled, and left his horn behind,
For husbands past their youth to find;
The nymph, who still with passion burn'd,
Was to a boiling fountain turn'd,
Where childless wives crowd every morn,
To drink in Acheloüs horn.
And here the father often gains
That title by another's pains.

Hither, though much against the grain,
The Dean has carried Lady Jane.
He, for a while, would not consent,
But vow'd his money all was spent:
His money spent! a clownish reason!
And must my lady slip her season?
The doctor, with a double fee,
Was bribed to make the Dean agree.

Here all diversions of the place
Are proper in my lady's case:
With which she patiently complies,
Merely because her friends advise;
His money and her time employs
In music, raffling-rooms, and toys;
Or in the Cross-bath seeks an heir,
Since others oft have found one there;
Where if the Dean by chance appears,
It shames his cassock and his years.
He keeps his distance in the gallery,
Till banish'd by some coxcomb's raillery;
For 'twould his character expose,
To bathe among the belles and beaux.

So have I seen within a pen,
Young ducklings fostered by a hen;
But, when let out, they run and muddle,
An instinct leads them, in a puddle;
The sober hen, not born to swim,
With mournful note clucks round the brim.

The Dean, with all his best endeavour,
Gets not an heir, but gets a fever.
A victim to the last essays
Of vigour and declining days,
He dies, and leaves his mourning mate
(What could he less?) his whole estate.

The widow goes through all her forms;
New lovers now will come in swarms.
O, may I see her soon dispensing
Her favours to some broken ensign!
Him let her marry, for his face,
And only coat of tarnish'd lace;
To turn her naked out of doors,
And spend her jointure on his whores;
But, for a parting present, leave her
A rooted pox to last for ever!

An Excellent New Ballad

Or, the True English Dean to be Hanged for a Rape

Our brethren of England, who love us so dear,
And in all they do for us so kindly do mean,
(A blessing upon them!) have sent us this year,
For the good of our church, a true English dean.
A holier priest ne'er was wrapt up in crape,
The worst you can say, he committed a rape.

In his journey to Dublin, he lighted at Chester,
And there he grew fond of another man's wife;
Burst into her chamber and would have caress'd her;
But she valued her honour much more than her life.
She bustled, and struggled, and made her escape
To a room full of guests, for fear of a rape.

The dean her pursued, to recover his game;
And now to attack her again he prepares:
But the company stood in defence of the dame,
They cudgell'd, and cuff'd him, and kick'd him down stairs.
His deanship was now in a damnable scrape,
And this was no time for committing a rape.

To Dublin he comes, to the bagnio he goes,
And orders the landlord to bring him a whore;
No scruple came on him his gown to expose,
'Twas what all his life he had practised before.
He made himself drunk with the juice of the grape,
And got a good clap, but committed no rape.

The dean, and his landlord, a jolly comrade,
Resolved for a fortnight to swim in delight;
For why, they had both been brought up to the trade
Of drinking all day, and of whoring all night.
His landlord was ready his deanship to ape
In every debauch, but committing a rape.

This Protestant zealot, this English divine,
In church and in state was of principles sound;
Was truer than Steele to the Hanover line,
And grieved that a Tory should live above ground,
Shall a subject so loyal be hang'd by the nape,
For no other crime but committing a rape?

By old Popish canons, as wise men have penn'd 'em,
Each priest had a concubine jure ecclesiae;
Who'd be Dean of Fernes without a commendam?
And precedents we can produce, if it please ye:
Then why should the dean, when whores are so cheap,
Be put to the peril and toil of a rape?

If fortune should please but to take such a crochet,
(To thee I apply, great Smedley's successor,)
To give thee lawn sleeves, a mitre, and rochet,
Whom wouldst thou resemble? I leave thee a guesser.
But I only behold thee in Atherton's shape,
For sodomy hang'd; as thou for a rape.

Ah! dost thou not envy the brave Colonel Chartres,
Condemn'd for thy crime at threescore and ten?
To hang him, all England would lend him their garters,
Yet he lives, and is ready to ravish again.
Then throttle thyself with an ell of strong tape,
For thou hast not a groat to atone for a rape.

The dean he was vex'd that his whores were so willing;
He long'd for a girl that would struggle and squall;
He ravish'd her fairly, and saved a good shilling;
But here was to pay the devil and all.
His troubles and sorrows now come in a heap,
And hang'd he must be for committing a rape.

If maidens are ravish'd, it is their own choice:
Why are they so wilful to struggle with men?
If they would but lie quiet, and stifle their voice,
No devil nor dean could ravish them then.
Nor would there be need of a strong hempen cape
Tied round the dean's neck for committing a rape.

Our church and our state dear England maintains,
For which all true Protestant hearts should be glad:
She sends us our bishops, our judges, and deans,
And better would give us, if better she had.
But, lord! how the rabble will stare and will gape,
When the good English dean is hang'd up for a rape!

In Sickness

'Tis true—then why should I repine
To see my life so fast decline?
But why obscurely here alone,
Where I am neither loved nor known?
My state of health none care to learn;
My life is here no soul's concern:
And those with whom I now converse
Without a tear will tend my hearse.
Removed from kind Arbuthnot's aid,
Who knows his art, but not his trade,
Preferring his regard for me
Before his credit, or his fee.
Some formal visits, looks, and words,
What mere humanity affords,
I meet perhaps from three or four,
From whom I once expected more;
Which those who tend the sick for pay,
Can act as decently as they:
But no obliging, tender friend,
To help at my approaching end.
My life is now a burthen grown
To others, ere it be my own.

  Ye formal weepers for the sick,
In your last offices be quick;
And spare my absent friends the grief
To hear, yet give me no relief;
Expired to-day, entomb'd to-morrow,
When known, will save a double sorrow.

The Day of Judgment

With a whirl of thought oppress'd,
I sunk from reverie to rest.
A horrid vision seized my head,
I saw the graves give up their dead!
Jove, arm'd with terrors, bursts the skies,
And thunder roars and lightning flies!
Amazed, confused, its fate unknown,
The world stands trembling at his throne!
While each pale sinner hung his head,
Jove, nodding, shook the heavens, and said:
"Offending race of human kind,
By nature, reason, learning, blind;
You who, through frailty, stepp'd aside;
And you, who never fell from pride:
You who in different sects were shamm'd,
And come to see each other damn'd;
(So some folk told you, but they knew
No more of Jove's designs than you;)
—The world's mad business now is o'er,
And I resent these pranks no more.
—I to such blockheads set my wit!
I damn such fools!—Go, go, you're bit."

Swift's Epitaph

Written by Himself

HIC DEPOSITUM EST CORPUS
JONATHAN SWIFT
HUJUS ECCLESIAE CATHEDRALIS
DECANI
UBI SAEVA INDIGNATIO
COR ULTERIUS LACERARE NEQUIT.
ABI, VIATOR,
ET IMITARE, SI POTERIS,
STRENUUM PRO VIRILI LIBERTATIS
VENDICEM.

HERE LIES THE BODY OF
JONATHAN SWIFT
OF THIS CATHEDRAL CHURCH
DEAN
WHERE SAVAGE INDIGNATION
CANNOT LACERATE HIS HEART ANYMORE.
TRAVELLER, GO,
AND IMITATE IF YOU CAN
HIS STRENUOUS VINDICATION OF
MAN'S LIBERTY.